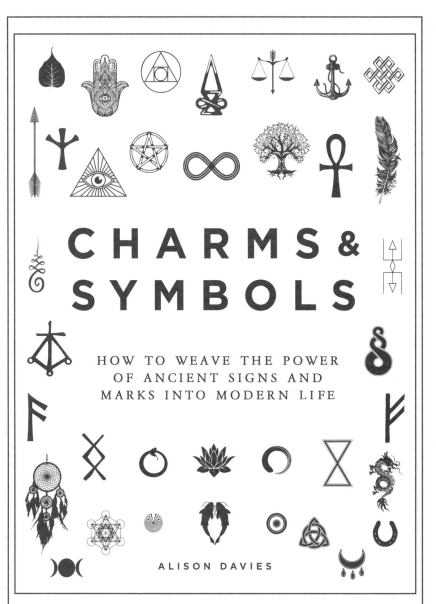

CHARMS & SYMBOLS

HOW TO WEAVE THE POWER OF ANCIENT SIGNS AND MARKS INTO MODERN LIFE

ALISON DAVIES

An Hachette UK Company
www.hachette.co.uk

First published in Great Britain in 2022 by Pyramid,
an imprint of Octopus Publishing Group Ltd
Carmelite House
50 Victoria Embankment
London, EC4Y 0DZ
www.octopusbooks.co.uk

Distributed in the US by
Hachette Book Group
1290 Avenue of the Americas
4th and 5th Floors
New York, NY 10104

Distributed in Canada by
Canadian Manda Group
664 Annette St.
Toronto, Ontario, Canada M6S 2C8

ISBN: 978-0-7537-3502-2

A CIP catalogue record for this book is available from the British Library
Printed and bound in Singapore

10 9 8 7 6 5 4 3 2 1

Publisher: Lucy Pessell
Designer: Hannah Coughlin
Editor: Sarah Kennedy
Editorial Assistant: Emily Martin
Production Controllers: Nic Jones and Lucy Carter

INTRODUCTION

Born from myth and legend and imbued with mystical connotations, it's easy to believe that symbols are just a work of the imagination. They exist as a key part of communication, and a way for us to understand the world. With deeply embedded concepts, which have evolved over the years, and are influenced by our experiences upon the earth, their meanings are many layered and sometimes universal depending on the type of symbol and where it occurs.

Some have their roots in nature and come from the sights and sounds that early humans experienced. They are the coiled shape of the tree as it twists in the breeze, the ebb and flow of the waves that lap at the shore. Some are more angular, bearing a physical presence that our ancestors came to associate with a certain kind of feeling or action. Take the warrior's arrow, bent on success, charged and ready to fly to secure a meal for the tribe. This was surely an emblem of survival and strength, and traced upon cave walls and carvings to signify victory.

Some symbols have been with us since birth and while we might not recognize their significance, we feel at home with them. The circle, with its ever flowing lines and gentle curve, is a shape that babies recognize and like because it feels safe and soothing – a fact that can be noted from the perfectly round faces of cuddly toys and dolls. On a more primal level, it connects us to the earth, to the cycles of life and the continual flow of the seasons. Then there are those symbols which form the basis of epic tales, stories told to bridge the gap between this world and the next, to explain the unexplained. The scarab is a good example of this, it's the sacred beetle that rolls the sun across the sky each day according to Egyptian folklore, and this goes some way to explain its message of rebirth and renewal. Such symbols may be influenced by myth, but there is always a kernel of truth at their heart, and a way to understand where their meaning comes from.

Today symbols are all around us. From the directions and road signs we see on our daily commute, to the more subliminal labels in advertising and literature. The flags that our countries carry as a mark of who we are and what we represent are some of the most powerful symbols, and the simple things, like a name tag to identify a role, are a badge that exudes authority.

This book looks at a selection of symbols from around the world. Charms, motifs, emblems and signs all have a place within these pages. While you might not believe in otherwordly influences, each symbol has been gifted with a type of energy, thanks to those who hold it in high regard and believe in its worth.

Once you have discovered the origins of the symbol and why it is important, you'll be able to connect with its meaning at a deeper level and use it in your own life in a positive way. From exercises in self-care, to meditation and techniques to help you relax and switch up your mindset, you'll see how you can use the symbol to improve wellness and help you manifest your best life.

Split into sections to help you identify the most effective symbol to work with depending on your needs, you can read the book from start to finish, or dip in when you need to, and let the right symbol find you. Once you begin to learn the secrets behind the signs and symbols, you'll gain a deeper understanding of your ancestors, who they were and how their influence has shaped your world. You'll also see the symbols at work in your own life and begin to value their importance. As humans we are forever seeking the truth and moving forward, and symbols can help us do this – from the ancient to the current, they have a place and a purpose in our world.

'As a plant produces its flower, so the psyche creates its symbols.'

Carl Jung

BALANCE
AND
CENTRING

CAIRN

PEACE,
RITUAL,
STILLNESS

Originating from the Scottish Gaelic word 'carn', meaning 'heap of stones', a Cairn is a pile of rocks stacked into a mound, which can be man-made or naturally formed. Used as markers in ancient times, these stone piles have been found all over the world, appearing on mountain sides, by lakes and rivers, in desert land and on some of the toughest terrains.

The Native Americans used them to mark battle sites and land boundaries, but they also believed that the stones were vehicles for transmitting prayer, and would place them in piles with incantations as a sacred act. Cairns have also been positioned to mark burial sites, and for their astrological influence, as they point toward the sun at a particular time of day. Some were built for ceremonial purposes while others were used during hunting expeditions.

While a Cairn can crop up anywhere, it is in Scotland that they're most commonly seen, dotting the landscape, and taking visitors back in time with their presence. According to folklore, Scottish clan leaders would create stone piles before going into battle. Each warrior would place a stone upon the stack and when he returned, he'd retrieve it so that the stones remaining became a memorial to those who had lost their lives.

One of the most famous and oldest, Clava Cairns, can be found near Inverness. It's a burial site and a monument, believed to be at least 4,000 years old.

It's popular practice to add a stone when you stumble across a Cairn, as a mark of respect for those who have gone before. Whatever the reason for building the Cairn, the act itself is symbolic and represents peace and balance. From harnessing the sun's power, to paying respect to your ancestors, the Cairn can help you find stillness within.

WORKING WITH CAIRN

Use the practice of building your own mini Cairn to help you find inner peace and balance.

- ❖ *You can build a small cairn as a table decoration, or in your garden, depending on the space and time you have.*
- ❖ *Start by gathering a selection of nicely shaped, somewhat flat, stones. If you've collected stones over the years from your travels you can use these, otherwise go on a hunt and find some that you like.*
- ❖ *Spend time wiping and smoothing each stone. Engage your senses as you do this and notice the way the stone feels along with its appearance.*
- ❖ *Slowly begin to build your Cairn by positioning each stone carefully to create the shape of your choice.*
- ❖ *If you prefer, add a stone a day and make a wish or say a short prayer or affirmation like 'I place this stone and find my balance'.*

UNALOME

JOURNEY,
ENLIGHTENMENT,
EXPLORATION

The intricate twists and turns of the Unalome chart a person's life upon the earthly plane. They show the journey that we go on from birth to enlightenment and the challenges that we face. Sometimes we have to deviate from the plan, go back on ourselves and even change direction, this is all present in the captivating swirls of the Unalome. One of the many symbols gifted to Buddha during his enlightenment, it appears in ancient texts and works of art to depict aspects of Buddhism and the voyage that each soul takes.

The journey begins at the centre of the base spiral, at birth, and then slowly unravels as we encounter hardship and suffering. Although the struggles of life are highlighted with this symbol, it is all about movement and finding the joy in each moment, so while we may face challenging situations, we continue onward and upward.

The criss-cross lines, show the personal path to enlightenment, and the changes that will help you get to where you want to be. The final straight line reflects a period of balance and wisdom; you have reached your goals and attained a sense of peace and understanding. Sometimes a Lotus Flower sits at the top of the Unalome, to symbolize reaching Nirvana.

Primarily this symbol is about spiritual awakening and the journey we must take to get to this point, but some believe it's a reflection of male and female energy, depending on which way the spirals face. When bent toward the left, it points to feminine energy and when veering to the right, masculine. However you perceive the Unalome, it is a powerful symbol that can be used to centre body, mind and spirit.

WORKING WITH
UNALOME

The best way to tap into the power of this symbol is to practise drawing it on paper. This can take some time to achieve but is well worth the effort.

- ❖ *To start, find a clear image of the Unalome, and trace over it with a dark pencil.*

- ❖ *Every day, spend five to ten minutes re-tracing the image.*

- ❖ *Treat this as a type of meditation, so put all of your focus into the pencil and the drawing. If your mind wanders, bring it back to the symbol.*

- ❖ *Once you have mastered drawing the symbol, think about each part of it and what it represents.*

- ❖ *Use this time to breathe and connect with how you are feeling. Think about your personal journey and how you can bring more joy into your life.*

ANCHOR

STRENGTH,
UNITY,
GROUNDING

The Anchor is a practical symbol with roots that stretch far back in history. The first anchors appeared in ancient Rome, around the 1st century, but similar symbols have been found on coins from ancient Greece. It's thought they were a way of honouring the god of the sea, Neptune. Some of the earliest known representations appear in ancient catacombs, as a mark of Christian faith, but while the Anchor bears a striking resemblance to the cross, it is not as overt. This made the Anchor the perfect way to identify other Christians during the Roman persecution. It soon became a secret symbol of faith and strength.

In later years, it took on a different role, becoming a staple tool for those at sea and a way to hold ships in place. When the anchor was released, it would grip onto the seabed, thanks to two sturdy flukes which look like arms. It was attached to a large chain which was fixed to the boat, and would hold the vessel securely, rooting it to the spot.

Because of its practical nature, the Anchor is associated with strength and security, but each part of the symbol has a specific meaning. The cross relates to those early Christian days and symbolizes a unity of spirit, the flukes represent the love between two people and how each one is connected. The crescent moon shape is associated with feminine energy, and some believe it represents the womb. In its entirety the Anchor has many different meanings. It's a reminder to stay anchored to your roots, to ground yourself and find strength from the simple things in life, like family and love. It's a symbol of opportunity and suggests that you have all the strength and courage you need to venture forth and achieve your dreams.

WORKING WITH ANCHOR

Use the energy of the Anchor to help you find balance and strength by combining movement, posture and breathing in this simple technique.

- ❖ *Stand with your feet-hip width apart, your shoulders relaxed and your weight balanced equally between each foot.*

- ❖ *Lengthen and extend your spine.*

- ❖ *Bend your knees and drop your weight into your lower legs; feel yourself securely anchored to the spot.*

- ❖ *Bounce for a moment and feel your connection to the earth.*

- ❖ *Bend as low as is comfortable for you, then draw in a long deep breath and imagine it coming up from the ground through each foot, into your legs and body.*

- ❖ *Return to a standing position, take a deep breath and say, 'I am balanced and anchored at all times'.*

HUNAB KU

H A R M O N Y ,
A L I G N M E N T ,
D U A L I T Y

The Hunab Ku is an ancient Mayan symbol which is associated with a deity known as the One God. The word 'Hunab' means 'One state of being' while Ku refers to 'God' so together they represent an all-encompassing force, more powerful than anything else. Some scholars have suggested that the term refers to the Christian God and was used by missionaries in South America to aid their cause. The name would have been something that the local people could understand, so it helped to make Christianity more acceptable.

The symbol, which also appears in ancient Aztec texts and upon ritual cloaks, was originally a rectangular design, but was later changed in the 1980s by a New Age guru named José Argüelles. He put his own slant on it, changing the shape and colours to enhance the meaning. The new design, which is circular and includes the opposing shades of black and white is often likened to the Chinese Yin and Yang symbol and embodies the same principles of duality and balance.

Today the Hunab Ku can be found in artwork, on prints, clothing and in jewellery. It's a popular design with a potent meaning. It brings opposites together, from male and female to dark and light, it becomes a bridge which unites these things and an emblem of harmony and balance. Embracing this symbol can help you find your centre and unite body and spirit. When life throws a curveball and everything seems upside down, the Hunab Ku can bring you into alignment with the universe and create a sense of peace.

WORKING WITH
HUNAB KU

Centre yourself with this breathing exercise that taps into the harmonious power of the Hunab Ku.

❖ *Focus on the Hunab Ku. Let your eyes soften and relax as you take in the image. Notice how the black and white shapes merge together to form the complete symbol.*

❖ *Close your eyes and picture the Hunab Ku at the centre of your chest.*

❖ *Place both hands palm down over your heart and take a deep breath in, then exhale.*

❖ *When you breathe in again, imagine you're inhaling white light infused with peace. As you breathe out, imagine you're exhaling any stress.*

❖ *Feel your body relax and continue to breathe in this way for a few minutes.*

OM

UNITY,
ACTIVATE,
CONNECTION

This widely used symbol and sound is thought to encompass all aspects of the universe. Associated with Hindu and Buddhist practices, it's a common mantra chanted during yoga, meditation sessions and also during prayers. From the 6th century onward, the written symbol was used as an inscription at the beginning and end of manuscripts.

The sound of Om, pronounced Aum, resonates deep within the belly, and activates the body's energy centres, known as chakras. At the heart of each syllable lies a sacred formula. Each letter has a meaning; the A stands for the waking state, U the dream state and M the unconscious state. When spoken aloud it unifies body, mind and soul, and brings all states of consciousness together.

The symbol is made up of curves, a crescent and a dot, and each marking relates to one of the three states. The bottom curve represents the waking state, the middle is the dreaming state and the upper curve is the unconscious state, while the crescent shape that sits on the top signifies illusion, the main obstacle which blocks us from achieving infinite wisdom. The dot right at the top is the fourth state of consciousness and represents the moment when we are finally connected to the Divine and at peace.

Om is most commonly associated with the Hindu god Ganesha; the curves in the symbol depict his elephant form. He is known as the deity who can remove all obstacles, and this links with Om's true purpose to align us to our higher self and let go of earthly concerns.

WORKING WITH OM

Use the power of Om to centre yourself.

---

* *Find a comfortable spot to sit and have a copy of the symbol in front of you.*
* *Think about the sound associated with it, and how each part fits with a specific marking on the symbol.*
* *Take a deep breath in from your belly and let the word 'aum' form in your mouth.*
* *Roll the sound out, and feel it resonate within as you exhale.*
* *Repeat the process, breathing in and then releasing the chant as you exhale.*
* *Do this for at least five minutes or until you feel totally relaxed and centred.*

OUROBOROS

CYCLES, REBIRTH, NEW BEGINNINGS

This powerful symbol appears in many forms throughout mythology. The word itself stems from ancient Greek and means 'tail devourer' and the symbol is most commonly associated with Greek and Egyptian folklore. It refers to a mythical serpent that is caught in a cycle of death and rebirth. This snake-like creature spends eternity devouring its own tail but is then born again, of itself. This never-ending loop is said to reflect the cycles of life

and that when we die, we are reborn into the afterlife. It also represents a unity between physical and spiritual matter, and infers that the natural order of life is to destroy and create in a timeless loop.

An early depiction of the symbol was found in a sacred text found in Tutankhamun's tomb, where it appeared twice, once at the head and once at the feet of Ra-Osiris. This link to the gods further enhanced its power and it became a symbol synonymous with chaos and creation.

To the alchemists it was a powerful tool that could free them from the endless cycle of death and rebirth, while the Gnostics, an ancient religious sect, saw it as a symbol of fertility and believed it represented heaven and earth, and the lines between the two.

Most commonly though, it is associated with the cycles of life and illustrates that for every death, there must be a rebirth of sorts and a new beginning. In this respect the Ouroboros can help us move forward, release the past and create a new and exciting future.

WORKING WITH
OUROBOROS

Use the endless cycle of the Ouroboros to calm and centre body and mind with this breathing exercise.

- ❖ *Find somewhere comfortable to sit where you won't be disturbed. Relax your shoulders and lengthen your spine to allow your diaphragm plenty of movement.*
- ❖ *Rest your hands on your lap, palms upward.*
- ❖ *Take a breath in, and as you inhale imagine you're taking in air through your right hand. It travels up the arm and around the body, filling your lungs and pumping your heart.*
- ❖ *As you exhale it travels down your left arm and is released through your left palm, to make a continual loop.*
- ❖ *Carry on breathing in this way for at least five minutes.*
- ❖ *Focus on the journey of the breath, and the gentle, rhythmic flow as you inhale and then exhale.*

SCALES OF JUSTICE

BALANCE,
FAIRNESS,
MEASURED

A common sight, standing proud outside courthouses around the world, the scales of justice represent the balance between right and wrong. They are a reminder that the legal system should remain fair, and that both sides will have their say. The scales are a symbol of justice and often depicted in the hands of the Roman goddess Lady Justice, also known as Dike among the ancient Greeks. The origins of this deity, and the link to the scales can

be found in ancient Egypt, and the realm of the goddess Maat. Known for her Ostrich feather, which she used in a judgement ceremony to the weigh the heart of the recently deceased. The feather would be placed on one side of the scales, and the deeds of the heart on another, together they would be weighed to find out which was heavier. The outcome would determine whether a soul was fit to pass onto the afterlife.

A symbol synonymous with truth, the scales have to come to mean balance and fairness in all things. They are a sign, particularly to those within the legal field, that both sides of the argument should be heard before any judgement is made.

Also associated with the star sign Libra, the scales encourage us to broaden our perception and see both points of view. Like Lady Justice, who makes no judgement but simply weighs the facts, we must be able to take a step back, look at things objectively and come to a measured conclusion. When we can do this, we will achieve a sense of balance.

WORKING WITH
SCALES OF JUSTICE

Use the scales to help you when you have to make a decision between two paths.

- ❖ *Stand with your arms out in front of you bent at the elbow, palms up.*

- ❖ *Imagine you are cupping the air lightly in each hand. Your arms should be equally weighted and balanced.*

- ❖ *Now take a couple of calming breaths and imagine that in each hand you hold a decision.*

- ❖ *Wait a few seconds and then notice which arm feels heavier. It might not be obvious, but one arm will ache more than the other, as your subconscious mind influences the outcome.*

- ❖ *Imagine letting go of this decision and leaving yourself holding the other one in both hands. How does this feel? If you feel lighter, and balanced, then you know this is the right course of action for you.*

FOCUS
AND
CLARITY

SHRI YANTRA

CLARITY,
FOCUS,
FULFILMENT

The Shri Yantra, also called the Queen of Yantras, is a sacred symbol used in Vedic traditions, and more specifically a branch of Hinduism known as the Shri Vidya school of tantra. This mystical design is a meditation tool used by ancient yogis, to enhance concentration and manifest desires. Like most yantras it's been around for thousands of years. The word 'yantra 'comes from the word 'yam' which means 'instrument' and 'tra' stems from 'trana' which means 'release from bondage'. The meaning as a whole suggests that yantras are tools for spiritual and emotional freedom.

The Shri Yantra is a powerful representation of the universe with the body of the divine goddess at its centre. Recreated on bark or paper, using petals and ash for the patterns, this symbol is commonly etched upon a copper plate, then blessed by priests who infuse it with a specific energy or intention.

Each part of the Shri Yantra has a meaning and represents a type of energy called Shakti. The outer square, which is T-shaped and comprised of 'gates' is associated with the earth element and represents emotions such as anger and fear. It's thought that meditating on this shape can help you defeat earthly passions.

The three inner circles relate to the past, present and future, while the lotus petals suggest fulfilment of hopes and dreams. Triangles also feature in the design and represent different concepts and energies, which work in unison.

With its complex geometry, the Shri Yantra combines beauty with mathematic ingenuity and powerful spiritual energy, making it the perfect tool to help you find clarity, focus and inner peace.

WORKING WITH
SHRI YANTRA

When you're seeking clarity and you need to clear your mind of clutter, this symbol can help. Simply tune into its energy and let the intricate patterns do the work.

❖ *Spend a few minutes focusing on the black and white image of the Shri Yantra.*

❖ *Relax your eyes and take in every detail.*

❖ *Breathe deeply and trace the pattern in your mind, going over each line and petal. Don't worry if your mind wanders, just bring it back to the image.*

❖ *When you're ready, close your eyes and imagine you're gazing at a cinema screen inside your head. Re-create the image upon the screen. See it flash up and hold it there for a few seconds.*

❖ *Slowly open your eyes, take a deep breath in and as you breathe out imagine you're expelling all the clutter from your mind.*

ARROW

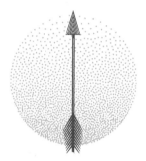

M O T I V A T I O N ,
D E C I S I O N ,
F O C U S

Arrows are a common sight and usually used as a way of pointing out a route, but there's more to these simple directional tools than meets the eye. The first arrows, which were used as weapons, were found in Africa almost 70,000 years ago. Cave paintings show that arrows were used around the world as a form of protection, and to hunt prey. To the ancient Greeks and Romans, arrows were the warrior's friend and used in battle, but they also had a softer connotation, with the introduction of Cupid, or Eros as he was called by the Greeks. In this guise, arrows became love darts able to incite feelings of lust and affection.

The arrow was the tool of choice for Native Americans, who hunted to survive the harsh landscape. Those early tribes would win food and keep their enemies at bay with the help of a sharpened arrowhead, and because of this it soon became associated with protection and strength. The freedom with which the arrow flew, and its speed, gave it energy and movement. Depending on the size and direction it was pointing, it would represent different things. An arrow to the left symbolized great power, to the right it meant protection and if it was pointing straight ahead, it was a symbol of positive action. An arrow facing down, was always synonymous with peace.

During the 19th century, the arrow's role as a weapon diminished, and the shaft gradually disappeared leaving only the triangular head, which is how the arrow became a symbol of direction.

Today we use the arrow as a guide to help us move forward, and make decisions. It's a symbol that sharpens the mind and provides motivation.

WORKING WITH
THE ARROW

Use the arrow in a simple breathing technique, which focuses the mind and energizes the body.

❖ *Stand or sit and lengthen your spine so that you can breathe deeply.*

❖ *Imagine that each inhale is a moving arrow of light, which starts at the base of the spine and travels up through your body, along your neck until it reaches your head.*

❖ *As you exhale, release the arrow and lengthen your outward breath.*

❖ *Continue to repeat this cycle for between 3 and 5 minutes.*

VEGVÍSIR

P R O T E C T I O N ,
G U I D A N C E ,
C O U R A G E

This ancient Norse symbol is thought to have originated in Iceland and, with its eight points, acts like a compass, bringing home those who are lost. The eight staves, all of which are decorated with runes at the end, point in different directions. The combination of these runes in a wheel binds their individual meanings together, like words in a sentence. The name, which is split into two Norse words, Vegur meaning way or path, and

Vísir meaning pointer or guide, captures the symbol's essence. These words derive their meaning from the same word as the English 'wise'. Sometimes the Vegvisir is enclosed in a circle which is decorated with runes, but there are many different versions, some more modern than others.

It's no surprise that the Vegvísir was a common feature on Viking boats. This mighty seafaring community spent long periods of time away from home, so were in need of spiritual assistance when it came to navigation. Sometimes the symbol would be carried or worn as an amulet, but more often it was daubed in blood upon the forehead. In this way it was thought to protect the person and keep them safe on their travels.

While the core meaning of the

Vegvísir is linked to travel, and keeping the wearer safe, a more modern interpretation casts the symbol as a guide, helping those in need of direction find the right path. It's a tool that can be used to focus the mind and provide spiritual support when facing life's challenges.

WORKING WITH VEGVÍSIR

Let the Vegvísir inspire you and guide you to the right path.

❖ *Print off a copy of the Vegvísir and place it on the table.*

❖ *Light a candle to illuminate your path, then place this in a holder on top of the symbol.*

❖ *Relax and gaze into the flame. Let your eyes soften and watch as it sways and flickers. Notice how the flame moves in different directions, sometimes growing bigger and brighter, and stretching both left and right.*

❖ *Allow yourself to daydream and to think about the kind of life you'd like and where you'd like to be in five years' time.*

❖ *Have fun with this and engage your imagination. Let the thoughts flow in and out of your mind.*

❖ *You may have a sudden burst of inspiration, or the germ of an idea. Make a note of anything significant and use it as a starting point to map out future plans.*

NTEASEE

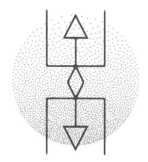

HARMONY,
COMPASSION,
EMPATHY

Nteasee is the Akan word for understanding, which is at the heart of this symbol's meaning. As part of the Adinkra, it belongs to the Asante people of West Africa, specifically the area now known as Ghana and Cote d' Ivoire. Printed on colourful cloth, Adinkra was a way to record proverbs, opinions and myths using intricate symbols. The material was fashioned into gowns and worn by nobility, usually at funerals. Each cloth was tailor-made for the wearer and would often tell a story which they could relate to. Today Adinkra is popular throughout the world, and easier to create using modern techniques and equipment, but the old ways of weaving and hand painting are still much loved and used.

Nteasee tells a story of co-operation. It's about overcoming differences and learning to come together. Even if you have opposing ideas, there's a sense that you can complement and learn from each other. Nteasee urges us to be more compassionate and understanding, particularly with those who go against us. It's a symbol that represents harmony and the meeting of minds, helping to improve clarity and focus.

Working with Nteasee can help you find common ground

with others, and even empathize with their plight. Use Nteasee to remind you to listen carefully before reaching a conclusion, whether it's listening to other people or to different voices within yourself when you are faced with a difficult decision.

WORKING WITH
NTEASEE

Use Nteasee as a decision-making tool when you have two different paths in mind.

❖ *The symbol has two arrows, one pointing up and one pointing down to reflect two different approaches. On a piece of paper, draw those two arrows pointing in opposite directions.*

❖ *Think about the issue that is troubling you, and the choices that you have. Each arrow reflects a choice. Above the top one, write the positives of this choice, and do the same beneath the bottom arrow.*

❖ *When you think about each choice, how do you feel? Nervous, excited, worried, confident? Write the word that sums this up above or below.*

❖ *Take a step back and look at the full picture. Breathe and allow the right choice to speak to you.*

TRIPLE MOON

TRANSITION,
GROWTH,
CHANGE

This pagan symbol, popular among followers of Wicca, depicts the shifting transitions of the lunar cycle. It highlights the three phases of the moon, as it moves from its waxing crescent position through to a full moon, and then back to its waning crescent form. Those who practice magic believe that each transition is associated with a different type of energy. Each stage also highlights an aspect of the triple goddess and because of this it's also called the triple goddess symbol. The waxing crescent moon relates to the 'maiden' in her first flourish of life, the full moon is the 'mother', vibrant and nurturing and the waning crescent moon is the 'crone' — wise, enigmatic and at her most powerful. The triple goddess symbol also refers to three deities who represent different elements of power which are interrelated.

While the triple moon symbol is often thought of as a modern invention, the meaning behind the symbol finds its roots in ancient times. The Greek goddess of the moon Hecate was first depicted as a triple deity in the 5th century BCE, and from then onward triads of goddesses were linked together and mentioned in ancient texts.

Three is at the heart of this symbol, and this number appears often in Celtic mythology. From the three stages of birth, life and death, to the past, present and future, it is associated with the eternal cycle of life, the wheel that continues to move in an everlasting loop. Each stage blends seamlessly into the next, just as life moves forward, and the moon continues its lunar cycle. The triple moon symbol is easy to relate to; it illuminates our path in life, making it the ideal choice for clarity and purpose.

WORKING WITH
TRIPLE MOON

Boost your energy levels and work with the phases of the moon by using this symbol as your guide.

- ❖ *Spend a few minutes breathing deeply to calm your mind, then gaze at the Triple Moon symbol.*

- ❖ *Consider where you are right now, and which phase you identify with the most. Are you about to embark on a new project and bubbling over with excitement? If so, you're at the waxing crescent moon stage. Perhaps your plans are coming to fruition, and your creative energy is blossoming, then you are at the full moon stage. If you are now looking back and evaluating what has gone before, then you are at the waning crescent moon stage.*

- ❖ *Whichever phase you find yourself in, take a moment to breathe and acknowledge it. Give thanks for where you are and what you have achieved so far.*

FEHU

SUCCESS,
EFFORT,
REWARD

Fehu is a key symbol in the runic alphabet known as the Futhark. This ancient writing system, which emerged around the 1st century AD, was popular throughout Europe with the Norse and Germanic tribes. Although the runes were used as a way to communicate, their deeper meanings are rooted in mythology. From the sound of the symbol when it is spoken to its shape, each rune embodies a principle and resonates within us.

Fehu is synonymous with wealth. When translated, it refers specifically to cattle ownership, which would have been an important indicator of success and abundance at the time. It's a rune of hard work, but it is fruitful because it produces results. Fehu suggests that if we want to progress, we need to put the effort in, and when we do the rewards will be so much greater and more enjoyable. Comfort and prosperity flow easily with this rune, and when it turns up in readings it's a sign to take a step back and enjoy your success.

Along with material wealth, Fehu is the rune of luck, but rather than some otherworldly force this good fortune is man-made. Much like the Norse tribes who worked the land and reaped the rewards,

Fehu implies that when you make your own luck, you're more likely to hold on to it. It's a symbol of attainment and working with its energy can help you focus on what you want, and how to get it.

WORKING WITH
FEHU

Let Fehu help you move forward by switching your mindset to one of success.

❖ *Picture the symbol in your mind. Look at the strong markings pointing upward – there are no curves or smooth edges, this is a determined, forceful image.*

❖ *Imagine that Fehu is the road to your success. See yourself standing on this road and look ahead in the distance. What do you see?*

❖ *Picture your goal as your final destination. Put in as much detail as you can. Then imagine walking toward this goal.*

❖ *Start slow, then pick up speed and move from a walk to a jog, then to a sprint. Feel the ground moving beneath your feet as you glide easily to your destination.*

❖ *Say 'I am focused and ready to succeed'.*

TRISKELION

UNITY,
INSPIRATION,
CYCLICAL

The history of this Celtic emblem dates back thousands of years, with its first discovery in 3200 BC. Etched into the entrance of a prehistoric tomb in Ireland, the Triskelion was a silent marker for one dead soul, but it's use is far from morbid. It is a popular symbol, widely used today in jewellery, artwork and pagan practices. Commonly associated with the Celtic tribes of central Europe and Britain, it was found carved into rocks, or adorning ancient churches and ruins, which says something of the deeply spiritual nature of these early civilizations.

The design comprises three interlocking spirals of the same size and is based upon the Archimedean spirals. The word Triskelion derives from the Greek 'Triskels' which means 'three legged', and in some versions three legs are used to create the symbol, rather than spirals. With its wheel-like shape and reference to legs, it's no surprise that the symbol is associated with movement, and in particular the passing of time. It signifies the cycles of life, and how we move through the stages of birth, death and rebirth.

The Triskelion is made up of three interlocking shapes, and the number three is significant when it comes to interpreting this symbol. From the three phases of life to the maiden, mother and crone aspects of the triple Goddess. Some believe the three grouping refers to the underworld, earth and heaven, or to the past, present and future. While all of these explanations differ, the underlying theme is unity and the sense that everything is connected and cyclical.

The Triskelion is a symbol that can help you move forward, and on to the next phase in your life. It can also help you look to the past, and your ancestors, for inspiration and balance.

WORKING WITH
TRISKELION

Tap into the energy of the Triskelion for clarity of purpose and inspiration.

- ❖ *Trace the Triskelion on a large piece of paper. Label each spiral, making one the past, one the present and one the future.*
- ❖ *Spend some time looking at the symbol and consider what each of the spirals means to you.*
- ❖ *What do you think about when you think of the past? What have you learned from your experiences so far? Write down a few words to sum this up.*
- ❖ *Now look at the present – what is important to you right now? How do you feel in this moment? Write some words to reflect this.*
- ❖ *Finally, look at the future – what do you want to achieve in the future? What kind of person would you like to be? Write a few words that sum up your future aims.*
- ❖ *Keep as a reminder of how far you've come, and where you are going.*

CREATIVITY

TRIANGLE

ENERGY, EMOTION, ACTION

The Triangle might be one of the simplest symbols to recreate, but it is also one of the most profound. It can be interpreted in many different ways and appears throughout history and in cultures around the world. The ancient Egyptians loved their triangles, as the pyramids will attest, and the Christians used the triangle as the basis for the Holy Trinity. The ancient Greeks saw the triangle as the Delta Glyph and a doorway. This was partly down to its shape and the opposing sides which formed an opening, and a gateway to divine wisdom. Peering from the tips of buildings, in ancient monuments and more modern architecture, the triangle is much loved and respected.

It is synonymous with the number three, as it has three edges and three vertices, a fact that was not missed by the Celts who based many of their more intricate symbols, like the Triskellion (pages 38–39), upon this shape. Threes are important when it comes to deciphering the Triangle and there are different meanings attributed to this shape. Popular theories suggest the Triangle represents past, present and future, and life, death and rebirth. The maiden, mother and crone are also referred to, but any significant group of three can be represented, which is what makes the symbol so important and relatable.

The triangle is also a symbol of masculine and feminine energy, depending on which way it points; if it points upward then masculine energy is active and if it's inverted, then feminine energy is the predominant force.

In alchemy the three elements of the triangle relate to body, mind and soul, as well as thought, emotion and action, which impact upon each other to create an outcome. In this guise the triangle can be used to tap into your innate creativity, to help you achieve your dreams.

WORKING WITH
TRIANGLE

Use the triangular power of three to motivate and inspire you.

❖ *Visualize a triangle in your mind. See it as a physical mountain that you must climb. You are standing at the bottom, gazing up.*

❖ *Think creatively and imagine that your goal is at the top of the mountain. Use your imagination and see it as a gleaming jewel that you must claim.*

❖ *In your mind create a way to reach the top of the mountain with ease, for example a magical rope, or winged shoes that fly you up there.*

❖ *Imagine how you will feel when you reach the summit. What kind of emotions will you experience? Use these feelings to power you on as you climb the mountain in your mind.*

❖ *To finish, say 'I use my thoughts and emotions to power my actions; I create my future'.*

SCARAB

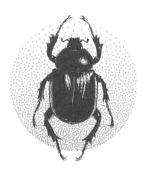

S T R E N G T H ,
R E N E W A L ,
R E B I R T H

Also known as the Kheper, this stunning beetle was a popular sight in ancient Egyptian works of art, and fashioned into seals and amulets. In nature, the beetle would lay its eggs in balls of dung, which it rolled carefully along the ground and deposited into one of its many burrows. The eggs, once hatched, would feast upon the dung from the inside out, emerging triumphant and transformed. It's for this reason that the Egyptians prized the scarab. The spontaneous birth was considered a miracle of nature, and so the beetle was associated with renewal and rebirth. Coming forth from nothing, also gave these creatures god-like status, and they were associated with the creator deity Atum. Creativity is a key theme linked to the scarab, thanks to the way it forms each dung ball and then uses it to produce new life, seemingly out of thin air.

The shape of their antenna and the way they gently roll each dung ball, also reminded the Egyptians of the sun as it travels through the sky. This gave rise to a number of stone tablets depicting the Scarab as sacred, the one who spun a path of light through the heavens.

As time moved on and the New Kingdom was born, it became a popular practice to place scarab amulets over the hearts of the deceased. Known as heart scarabs, they played an important role in the soul's journey to the afterlife by protecting the individual from false testimonies against them, while their deeds were being weighed against the feather to determine if they were worthy of rebirth.

A symbol imbued with life-giving energy, the Scarab can help when you need a fresh start, or if you're seeking a new beginning. It can also ignite your creative spark.

WORKING WITH SCARAB

Use the creative energy of the Scarab for motivation and to help you get started when you have a project in mind.

❖ *On a piece of paper, draw a large circle to represent both the ball of dung and the sun that the scarab rolls through the sky.*

❖ *In the centre of the paper, in a few words, sum up your idea or project.*

❖ *Around the outside of the circle write a number of actions that you can put in place which will help you move toward your goal. Anything from buying materials, to getting a mentor, or taking a course.*

❖ *Position the drawing somewhere where you will see it every day.*

❖ *Mark off each thing that you do, as you do it, and turn the image each time to represent you moving toward your goal.*

DENKYEM

FLEXIBILITY,
POWER,
ADAPTABILITY

The Denkyem is an Adinka symbol, which was originally produced by the Gyaaman clans of the Brong region in Ghana. Adinka is cotton cloth stamped with symbols which relate to the myths and proverbs of the Akan people. The symbols were developed over time to express opinions and even chart historical events, while some are simply abstract shapes used to convey a concept. The word Adinka means goodbye, a nod to the original use of the cloth at funerals and religious ceremonies. Eventually these cleverly crafted symbols were daubed on pottery, used on metalwork and more recently seen in architecture. As other tribes contributed to the Adinka its variety grew in size, and more shapes were added to reflect different cultures and portray folk tales and beliefs.

The Denkyem is the Adinka symbol for crocodile and captures the essence of this powerful beast. Believed to embody magical traits because of its ability to live in water but breathe air, the crocodile is synonymous with adaptability. A fearsome predator, with a quick-thinking mind, the crocodile also carries an air of mystery, which adds to its allure. Known for its ability to thrive in almost any environment, this creature is common in African myths and legends and was deeply valued by Ghanaian society. Because of this the Denkyem is a symbol of creativity, flexibility and power, and is a source of inspiration for many people, making it a popular tattoo choice.

Working with Denkyem can help you find ways to be flexible, and to approach problems in a more creative way when faced with challenging circumstances.

WORKING WITH DENKYEM

Tune into the energy of the Denkyem when you need to be flexible and creative in your thinking.

---

* *Study the shape of the symbol until you feel you know it well enough to recreate it.*

* *Fill a bowl with water and add a few drops of lavender essential oil. This lovely uplifting scent helps to calm and relax the mind, allowing creativity to flow.*

* *Dip your finger in the water, then trace the shape of the Denkyem onto your forehead.*

* *Go over the shape a few times with your finger, but don't worry if it isn't exact.*

* *Let the water be absorbed into your skin and inhale the floral aroma.*

* *Repeat the affirmation 'Like crocodile, I adapt and go with the flow'.*

DRAGON

WISDOM, GOOD FORTUNE, POWER

One of the most popular and prolific symbols of ancient China, the Dragon is associated with power, wisdom and good fortune. Creeping around doorways and windows and emblazoned on the robes of emperors, this mighty beast was a favourite marking, often carved into jade and other precious materials. While it appears in literature and ancient scriptures, the origins go back much further, with the discovery of carved dragons in excavations from the Hongshan dynasty as early as 4500–3000 BCE. Some historians believe the first mention of the Chinese dragon was in folklore associated with the rainbow. After the rain, the sun would emerge and bring with it the 'serpent of the sky' – a colourful, snake-like being which eventually morphed into a dragon.

Originally an ungainly beast, the dragon of old was composed of other animal parts. In some descriptions it had the claws of an eagle, the scales of a carp, the ears of an ox and the belly of a frog. Historians believe this amalgamation represented a union between several ancient tribes who had different animal totems. Over the years, this image evolved into a more elegant and pleasing version.

Thought to dwell in water, or rain clouds, the dragon was often accompanied by thunder and lightning. This gave it the auspicious mantle of 'bringer of the water', which was a vital source of life to the ancient people. Because of this, the dragon secured its place in Chinese culture, appearing in stories and plays as a fortuitous creature that could be called upon in times of need.

A symbol that will help you ignite your imagination and find the fire to fuel your passions, the Dragon can also help you follow your heart and make creative choices.

WORKING WITH
DRAGON

Ignite your creative spark, using the energy of the Dragon in this simple guided meditation.

- ❖ *Find a place where you won't be disturbed, switch off your phone, close the door and breathe.*
- ❖ *Place both hands just below your navel. Take a long breath in, then exhale through your mouth, making a 'swooshing' sound.*
- ❖ *Notice how your hands move up and down with every breath.*
- ❖ *Picture a tiny flame in your belly – this is your creative spark. With every breath that you take it gets bigger and brighter.*
- ❖ *Take your time and focus on extending each breath. Let the flame expand until eventually it reaches up, along your throat and comes out as you exhale, like dragon's breath.*

KORU

HARMONY,
NATURE,
UNDERSTANDING

The Koru, meaning loop or coil, is highly revered by the Maori, the indigenous people of New Zealand. It's at the heart of many of their famous designs and tribal tattoos, and an integral part of their culture. An ancient symbol, the Koru has been found in some of the earliest Maori dwellings dating back thousands of years. It decorates the rafters of the central platform of the Marae, an important meeting house where tribes congregate to discuss law,

ethics and religion, and is a key feature of Moru, a type of body art.

Nature, and all this encompasses, is central to the Maori way of life. Their spiritual practice focuses on the earth and its elements, including the sun, water and soil, and this forms the basis for many Maori rites and rituals. The Koru, finds its roots in the Silver Fern, which grows in abundance in the forests of New Zealand. Associated with growth, the first fronds of this fern mark the beginning of a new season.

The swirl of the Koru depicts the young frond slowly unfurling, while the gentle curling movement which comes from the centre is associated with the changeable nature of life, making the Koru a symbol of creativity and renewal. Often used in sacred artwork, the

Koru offers enlightenment and an understanding that at every stage of life there is the opportunity for rebirth. Over the years, this image has been associated with Maori culture and the powerful relationship between nature and humans. It's also a symbol synonymous with harmony and is often gifted to young couples when they get engaged or married, to signify a joyful union.

WORKING WITH KORU

Use the Koru to help you harness the creative, life-giving force of nature.

- *The circular swirl of the Koru brings you back to the central point if you trace it with your finger. It's a sign that all things must return to their place of origin, and the source of all creativity – the earth.*
- *If you're struggling with anxiety, take a moment to regroup and find balance.*
- *Spend some time in nature, whether in your garden, local park or further afield.*
- *Sit or stand and breathe in your surroundings.*
- *Imagine that with every breath, you draw strength from the earth. Feel this energy travelling through the soles of your feet until it finds your heart, then see it as a golden whirling Koru in the centre of your chest.*

ANSUZ

AGILITY,
CREATIVITY,
EXPRESSION

Ansuz is a powerful symbol, and one of 24 runes which form the Nordic alphabet. The runes are a set of letters which early Germanic tribes used as a form of communication. Known as the Futhark, they originate from ancient Italic alphabets used in 1st century CE by Mediterranean peoples. This, coupled with the influence of sacred symbols and carvings from early Germanic tribes, helped to shape the runes of today.

According to Norse legend, the runes were a gift to the god Odin, given in return for his blood sacrifice. For nine days and nights, he hung from the World Tree, otherwise known as Yggdrasil. Gazing down into the Well of Urd, he received visions and psychic messages, the final one being the lost alphabet of the runes. These carefully crafted symbols were more than just a way of communicating, they gave voice to the unspoken, helping to shape words and wield power. They were magical and could be used in rituals and spells.

Ansuz is the fourth rune in the collection, and the one that's specifically associated with Odin. As such, it represents breath as a life-force, the power of words and the ability to name things — something which was important to the ancient Norse people, as they believed it helped to bind evil spirits and break curses.

The name itself means 'god', but the deeper meaning is one of communication, of using words to organize and provide order. The influence of Odin gives this rune further magical power. According to legend, he gave the first humans breath, and with that came mental agility, and creativity.

This rune is the perfect choice for those wishing to express themselves, whether that's through literal forms like poetry or journaling, or in the way they deal with others and the world around them.

WORKING WITH
ANSUZ

Use the power of Ansuz to ignite your creativity.

❖ *Take a candle and using a pin, carve the Ansuz symbol into the wax.*

❖ *As you do this, think about the symbolism of the shape and what it represents. Consider all the areas of your life where you could be more creative. Ask yourself – how can I communicate more effectively? What do I need to do to express myself creatively? Then think of ways in which you could do this.*

❖ *When you've finished carving, light the candle and gaze into the flame.*

❖ *Take a deep breath in and as you breathe out, imagine a spark igniting just above your navel. This spark grows into a flame, which fuels your creative energy.*

❖ *Continue to focus on your breathing and let any words, thoughts, or ideas flow into your mind.*

MAN IN THE MAZE

ACCEPTANCE,
JOURNEY,
IMAGINATION

This elaborate maze, which is made of seven concentric circles, is associated with the Tohono O'odham nation, a Native American tribe from Central Valley, Arizona. Although it's a part of their mythology, it has been adopted by other tribes as its meaning is universal. Making its first appearance in basket weavings as early as the 1900s, it's still a popular symbol today, frequently seen in Native American jewellery designs.

The maze is a labyrinth, which we must navigate to join our ancestors in spirit. The middle point at the start is thought to represent humankind, and the point at which we're born. It is then up to us to walk the path and face each challenge that life presents, working our way through the twists and turns until we reach the centre, and the final moment of enlightenment.

The Tohono believe that I'itoi, an elder and spiritual figure, resides within the maze, both at the start and at the very centre, when we reach the end of our journey. The Gila River Indian community, known as the Akimel O'odham, believe the Man in the Maze is their creator, and he is called Se:he or Elder Brother. While the names vary, the meaning of the maze remains the same. It symbolizes our journey upon the earth, and the many trials and tribulations we face. It also illustrates that we create our own destiny, and that with a little imagination, we can walk the maze and find our true calling. When we finally reach the centre of the labyrinth, we are able to look back with acceptance, and give thanks for what we've learned and the life we've created.

WORKING WITH
MAN IN THE MAZE

Let the Man in the Maze help you embrace the flow of life, and the twists and turns of fate.

❖ *Create your own mini labyrinth using pretty stones and crystals to mark out the design. It doesn't have to be complicated. You can base it on the Man in the Maze or create something simpler. It's more important that you have fun with the design. This is about tapping into your creativity and embracing the flow wherever it takes you.*

❖ *You can make the pattern outside in your garden, or create something that you can use as a table decoration.*

❖ *Once you have come up with a pattern you like, sit for a moment and enjoy your design.*

❖ *Think about what this represents and how life is like a labyrinth. Look at the highs and lows as part of a beautiful pattern that you are creating here on earth.*

INNER PEACE
AND LOVE

ENSO

OPENNESS,
CONNECTION,
FOCUS

The Enso is an enigmatic symbol which finds its roots in Japanese calligraphy. Originally an art form that came from 28th century BC China but was imported to Japan around the 5th century AD, calligraphy was the domain of Buddhist monks and nuns, who perfected the art as part of their practice. As such, the gentle brushstrokes held a Zen influence, which has evolved over time.

The Enso is a not-so-perfect circle, achieved with only one brushstroke, making it both easy and hard to master. Those who attempt to create one must focus their mind and be present in what they are doing, yet still remain fluid and able to let go. Perfecting this balance of polar opposites is not an easy feat, and once the Enso has been completed it cannot be changed, for there is only one moment of creation. The word itself means 'circle' or 'circular form' which in turn means a hole that is both empty and full at the same time, depending on how you choose to look at it. This fits with the Zen approach to life, which suggests that 'form is void and void is form'.

The Enso is a sacred symbol in Zen Buddhism, and it has a many-layered meaning, being everything and nothing all at once.

It is the circle of life, the beauty of imperfection, the art of focus coupled with that of letting go. It is creativity in full flow, and to those artists who have experienced the Enso, it is a moment of openness and connection.

WORKING WITH
ENSO

Use the Enso as a meditation tool to calm the mind. It will help you engage with and find joy in the present moment, particularly if you're going through a tough time.

- *You'll need an artist's fine paintbrush, some black paint and a sheet of white paper.*
- *Spend a few moments breathing and focus on the whiteness of the page in front of you.*
- *Bring the image of the circle into your mind. See yourself completing the full circle with one swift brushstroke.*
- *Dip the brush into the paint, then take a long breath and count for four beats.*
- *As you exhale, touch the tip of the brush to the paper, then without thinking too much create the swirl of the circle in one graceful stroke.*
- *Remove the brush and gaze at your creation.*

PIKORUA

BONDS,
CONNECTION,
UNITY

A relatively new symbol in Maori culture, the Pikorua, often referred to as the 'twist' has many variations. The original, which could be described as a figure of eight with a small loop at the top and a larger one at the bottom, requires special tools to create, which is why it's believed to be more recent. Some variations include two, three and even four twists. While there are deviations, it's thought that the original shape is based upon the pikopiko fern which grows in the shadiest parts of the New Zealand bush. An important food source for the Maori people, it's also a symbol of unity.

The Pikorua's main theme is connection and it signifies the strong bonds we create with one another. When two people meet, their souls join, and together they face the twists and turns of life. Sometimes destiny pulls them apart, and sometimes it brings them back together. The Pikorua represents this journey. While this lends itself to lovers, it's also a symbol which can be used for an individual's life path, which may curve and bend with the choices that they make, and it's used to bring family members together and cement friendships. It highlights the connection that we have with loved ones, even those who have passed on to the afterlife. The Pikorua acts as a reminder that wherever we are, we are always together in spirit.

Working with the Pikorua can help you combat feelings of loneliness and isolation by reaffirming your connection to friends and loved ones.

WORKING WITH
PIKORUA

Draw on the loving energy of this symbol by combining it with crystal therapy.

❖ *Place a drawing of the Pikorua on the table in front of you.*

❖ *Pop a piece of rose quartz on top of the symbol and leave it overnight. This gentle stone exudes loving energy and, combined with the energy of the symbol, it will help you open your heart and be more loving to yourself and others.*

❖ *Retrieve the rose quartz the next day and hold it over the centre of your chest for a few minutes.*

❖ *As you breathe in, imagine you're inhaling the lovely pink energy of the stone. You should feel a warm sensation in your chest which spreads outward.*

❖ *Carry the stone with you for self-healing and to enhance loving vibes.*

CONCH SHELL

HOPE,
PURITY,
FAITH

This beautiful pink-tinted shell is revered around the world. The conch itself is a type of mollusc that comes out at night to feed and belongs to the Strombidae family. In India, the conch is referred to as the 'shankha' and first mentioned in an ancient text around 1000 BCE. Hindu myths and legends cite the shell as Lord Krishna's favoured instrument. It's thought he blew into it to announce the start and end of battles, and it is also used in Hindu rituals. The direction of the shell is important too, left pointing ones are used as objects of prayer and to hold holy water, while the right pointing shells, which are usually white, are used in rituals to honour the Buddha.

The Om sound that the shell emits when blown, is also significant and associated with Lord Vishnu, the Hindu god of sound. For this reason, it's believed to be a symbol of purity and is often kept in the household as a sacred object. In Buddhism, the conch represents the lilting and harmonious voice of the Buddha, and is one of eight auspicious symbols, called the Ashtamangala. Associated with hope, faith and courage, it is believed that blowing into the shell can help you attain these qualities.

A symbol that is linked to femininity, creativity and hope, the conch has many connotations, but at its heart, it represents purity and the beauty of the natural world. Tapping into its power will help you find inner peace and stillness in the midst of chaos.

WORKING WITH
CONCH SHELL

The conch is primarily associated with water and working with this element can help you to release pain and restore inner peace.

- ❖ *Fill a bowl with warm water. Add a sprinkling of sea or Epsom salts – both help with detoxification and eliminating negativity.*

- ❖ *Take a cup and scoop up some of the water. Imagine you're using a conch shell for this process.*

- ❖ *Start with your arms and let the water trickle from the cup onto your skin. Gently bathe each arm and as you do, imagine you're washing away impurity and letting any worries be absorbed into the water. You can do the same with your legs and feet.*

- ❖ *This bathing ritual is about self-care and nurturing. It gives you the time you need to release negative energy, so that you can move forward with optimism.*

BODHI LEAF

AWAKENING,
WISDOM,
KNOWLEDGE

The Bodhi leaf is an important symbol in Buddhism. It belongs to the fig tree, now known as the Bohdi or Buddhi tree. It was beneath its canopy of branches that the Nepalese prince Siddhartha Gautama sat while meditating for 49 days. He achieved his quest for enlightenment on the final day, and in that moment, he became the Buddha, and the humble fig tree became the Bodhi tree.

When the Buddha gazed up into the leaves and received infinite peace and knowledge, the spiritual path known as Buddhism was born. It's thought that afterwards, he gave thanks to the tree and the leaves for sustaining him during his journey and as a mark of respect remained staring up into the branches for another week. Today, in Bodh Gaya, a descendant of the original Bodhi tree still stands, marking this significant moment.

This symbol is also associated with the Hindu god Vishnu, who is depicted peering from the foliage of the Bodhi tree. He is a key deity in the Hindu religion, who also found spiritual succour sitting among the leaves. In nature too, the leaf has a role to play, providing sustenance to the elephant, the sacred animal of India. It's no surprise then that the

Bodhi leaf is a symbol of infinite wisdom and knowledge. It's a reminder that with hard work, diligence, and meditation, it is possible to achieve self-awareness and an awakening of sorts. It's believed that simply gazing upon the leaf, and letting its simplicity focus your mind, can help you attain a sense of enlightenment.

WORKING WITH
BODHI LEAF

Use the image of the Bodhi leaf and tree to help you during meditation to calm and centre the mind.

❖ *Find a picture of a Bodhi leaf and stare at it for a few minutes. Take in everything you can about its appearance. Look at the size, shape and markings, and the changes in colour. Imagine what it would feel like to hold the leaf in your hands.*

❖ *Place your finger somewhere upon the leaf and trace the outline a few times, then close your eyes and recreate the leaf in your mind.*

❖ *Picture yourself sitting beneath the Bodhi tree. Imagine you are wrapped in the foliage, cloaked in many Bodhi leaves.*

❖ *Breathe deeply and inhale the serenity.*

❖ *Let thoughts and feelings flow in and out of your mind and bring your focus gently back to the leaves.*

KAPEMNI

PEACE,
STABILITY,
JOY

'As above, so below' is the motto of the simple but timeless Kapemni. Otherwise known as the Lakota symbol, because of its association with the Lakota tribe of Native Americans. It represents the sun and the earth and the meeting of these two entities. The upper inverted triangle is the sun and the stars, while the bottom triangle which resembles a tipi, is the earth reaching up to the sky. Together they meet at a central point and become one.

The Lakota tribe, who lived on the Great Plains of North America, looked to the stars for inspiration and would study and map the constellations. They also studied the land and charted the dips and valleys, the mountains and the wildlife. From their musings, they came to the conclusion that the earth mirrored the night sky and created the symbol to illustrate this, but the Kapemni was more than just a drawing. To the Lakota it was a star map, with two vortexes that joined together in 3D. They believed that the symbol was a doorway, a portal between the spiritual and physical worlds. They used the Kapemni as a tool to determine where the sun was at any given point in the sky, and this helped them plan when to perform rituals and ceremonies.

A symbol with many interpretations, at its heart is connection; the way the earth interacts with the sun and stars and the way they mirror each other. It shows how earthly spirits connect with the heavens and send their prayers up to the sky. The Kapemni can help us connect with the natural world, and find peace, stability and joy in our surroundings.

WORKING WITH KAPEMNI

Use the Kapemni to help you connect with the natural world and engage your senses.

❖ *Stand barefoot on a patch of grass.*

❖ *Spend a few moments connecting with the earth. Feel the blades of glass graze your feet. Feel your soles press into the earth.*

❖ *Stretch your legs out into an inverted V shape, then take a deep breath in and stretch your arms up into the air.*

❖ *As you exhale, stretch your arms further apart to form a V shape.*

❖ *Close your eyes and tilt your face to the sun. Feel the warmth of the rays kiss your skin.*

❖ *Say 'As above, so below', and repeat this affirmation a few times.*

LOTUS

PATIENCE,
PEACE,
FORTITUDE

The beautiful lotus flower is a symbol of purity and peace. It is recognized around the world as an emblem of enlightenment. The ancient Egyptians associated it with their sun god Ra because of the way the petals opened beneath the sun's rays and followed its path through the sky. To the ancient Greeks it was a symbol of purity and innocence. Lotuses were found in Vedic texts as far back as 1400 BC, they were the flower of choice for Hindu gods who were often pictured holding them, while Buddha was a fan of sitting among the pretty blooms.

The lotus is a symbol of endurance in many cultures because of the way it grows. It thrives, despite finding it's home in muddy waters. The flower detaches itself from the mire to rise beneath the sun and blossom. This is a lesson of nature, illustrating that whatever situation we find ourselves in, we can rise above it and find some joy. The tenacity of this flower doesn't end here, according to fossil records it managed to survive the Ice Age, when many lesser plants became extinct. With this in the mind, the lotus truly is a symbol of strength and fortitude.

A particularly beautiful bloom which flowers one petal at a time, it's associated with patience. This fits perfectly with the Buddhist way of thinking, and highlights the path to enlightenment, which is also taken one step at a time. The golden centre of the flower relates to the moment of enlightenment, when inner peace has finally been reached.

A sacred flower with many meanings, the lotus captures the spirit of life, and as such has earned the mantle 'Womb of the World'.

WORKING WITH
LOTUS

Enjoy a moment of stillness with the help of the lotus symbol.

- ❖ *Sit on a cushion, with your legs folded if you can. Make sure you are comfortable.*
- ❖ *Close your eyes and bring your attention to the rise and fall of your chest.*
- ❖ *Take a deep breath in and hold for four beats, then as you breathe out count for another four beats.*
- ❖ *Continue to breathe in this way, counting out four slow beats as you inhale and exhale.*
- ❖ *Imagine you are sat within the sacred lotus. The petals envelope you, and you feel totally at peace.*
- ❖ *When you inhale, you breathe in the sweet scent. As you exhale, the petals slowly move toward you.*
- ❖ *Know that you are safe and at peace, cocooned within the heart of the flower.*

INTUITION

FEATHER

WISDOM,
HONOUR,
INTUITION

The feather is a widely used symbol in Native American mythology, acknowledged by all tribes, representing the link between heaven and earth. Imbued with the power of the bird that it came from, it is associated with honour, valour and wisdom. When young braves fought in battle, or displayed courage, they were often awarded a feather as a symbol of power. Eagle feathers, in particular, were considered the most auspicious, but owl feathers also held sacred medicine.

To the Cherokee, who once occupied several south-eastern states of America and were one of the largest tribal groups, the owl was revered. Taking centre-stage in their creation myth, which explains how the world came into being, the owl played a key role. According to the creation myth, when the earth was born, the animals lived in a realm called Galunlati. They were charged with watching over the creatures on earth for seven days and nights, but only the owl and the cougar stayed awake long enough to fulfil this task. As a reward, they were gifted with the ability to see in the dark. Owls also have eyes at the front of their head, a fact that the Cherokee believe links to us and the way we see the world.

Feathers, whether from eagles or owls, were seen as a supreme blessing, and often held above someone's head, as a way of wishing them health and happiness. Also used to adorn the sacred pipe, which is associated with the Great Spirit, they were an inherent part of ceremonies and rituals to promote peace.

In western culture, the feather is seen as a link between this world and the next, and considered a sign of love from those in the spirit realm. It symbolizes wisdom and honour, and can help you release fear and tune into your intuition.

WORKING WITH
FEATHER

Restore and rejuvenate body and mind using the power of the Feather to cleanse your aura.

* *The aura is the force field around the body, which often becomes clogged with negative energy.*

* *Hold a feather in your dominant hand, close your eyes and breathe deeply.*

* *Start at the top of your head and gently flick the feather back and forth.*

* *Continue with this movement, taking it around your body and down each leg.*

* *As you do this, picture yourself standing in a shower of white light which absorbs pain and imbues you with vitality.*

HECATE'S WHEEL

REBIRTH, RENEWAL, SELF-DISCOVERY

Hecate was the powerful Greek goddess of the crossroads. Queen of the witches, she was associated with magic and prophecy and also a triple goddess, meaning she symbolized the three elements of womanhood – maiden, mother and crone. One of the older deities, she had a strong following, with many temples and statues built in her honour. She could be called on for protection and summoned at the dead of night by a crossroads. Although she could appear as a beautiful young woman, the wrinkled crone was her favourite guise and one that most people associated with her.

Her wheel was an early symbol relating to her power as the triple goddess. It first emerged on tablets dating back to the 1st century and has since been adopted by the Wiccan tradition. At its heart is a labyrinth, which is a serpent that swirls from three directions, a nod to Hecate's triple goddess status. The labyrinth serpent is a symbol of rebirth and renewal. Each whirling maze leads to the sacred centre, which is believed to represent divine thought.

The symbol as a whole signifies a journey, the inner quest for knowledge and self-discovery. The influence of Hecate implies this might be an intuitive journey, where the querent uses the innate psychic skills associated with this deity to move forward. The wheel represents action and movement, and the central focal point is the destination, where all the power of the universe resides.

WORKING WITH
HECATE'S WHEEL

Let Hecate's Wheel ignite your intuition with this simple exercise.

- ❖ *Print an image of this symbol on a large sheet of paper. You'll need to make it as big as possible, so that you have plenty of room to traverse the twists and turns of the maze with your finger.*
- ❖ *Spend a few minutes gazing at the central point of the maze. This is the seat of your intuition. Say 'I have all the answers I need within'.*
- ❖ *Place your finger on the outer wall of the maze at any point, and begin to follow the circle around.*
- ❖ *Give this all of your attention. If your mind wanders, bring it back to the maze and start again.*
- ❖ *When you reach the centre, repeat the affirmation 'I have all the answers I need within'.*

DREAMCATCHER

SAFETY,
RELAXATION,
PROTECTION

A charm for dreamers and those seeking restful slumber, the dreamcatcher is a Native American symbol, which most likely originates from the Ojibwe tribe. Known as 'asabikeshiinh' in the local tongue, which means 'spider', this ornate wall hanging catches good dreams and expels bad ones. According to Ojibwe legend, sacred Spider Woman was always on hand to look after children, particularly at night, when she would chase away their nightmares. As the tribe spread, it became impossible for her to watch over every child, so instead she petitioned the help of the women, asking them to weave a spider's web to hang above the bed. The web, which was woven over a willow hoop, kept the children safe as they slept, and stole away bad dreams.

Each part of the dreamcatcher is significant and tells a story. The circular frame represents Mother Earth and the continual cycle of life. It also symbolizes the sun and the moon, and their journey through the sky. The web at the heart of the catcher is where the most potent medicine lies. It filters good dreams and visions through the central point, and ensnares the bad ones, then in the morning when the sun hits the web, they melt away. Some traditions believe that the good dreams fall from the web and form the feathers that hang at the bottom, from here they drip into the dreamer's mind. Other variations suggest it's the bad dreams that are filtered through the central hole, but the outcome is still the same, and the sleeper is safe in slumber.

Dreamcatchers can help you work with your dreams in a positive way, and if you're struggling to sleep, they're the perfect antidote.

WORKING WITH
DREAMCATCHER

Let the power of the dreamcatcher ease you into sleep, and help you relax.

- ❖ *Before you go to sleep, take some time to tap into the power of the dreamcatcher symbol.*

- ❖ *Close your eyes, breathe deeply and picture a spider's web in your mind. See it shining in the sunlight, a beautiful intricate pattern that glitters.*

- ❖ *Imagine it hanging above your bed, protecting you, and bathing you in the first rays of the morning sun. Feel the warmth upon your skin and feel your muscles relax.*

- ❖ *Know that you are safe and able to drift to sleep, and that your dreams are gifts from the subconscious mind.*

EYE OF PROVIDENCE

PROTECTION,
GUIDANCE,
FORTUNE

The Eye of Providence, also known as the All-Seeing Eye, is a striking and powerful symbol which depicts an eye, framed with light and encased in a triangle. It first appeared in a painting by the Italian Jacopo Pontormo where it was suspended above the head of Jesus Christ. Entitled 'Supper at Emmaus' the painting was created in 1525 for the Carthusians, a religious order belonging to the Roman Catholic church. While there are many religious connotations to this symbol, it's thought its origins go back much further to ancient cultures like the Egyptians who loved eye symbology and used similar designs for the Eye of Horus and the Eye of Ra. Buddha too was referred to as 'the eye of the world'.

In Christianity, the symbol is thought to represent the watchful eye of God upon humanity. It's associated with Divine Guidance and has a protective influence. There's also a sense of foreboding, in that God, the supreme being, sees everything we say and do, and so we must account for our actions as nothing goes unnoticed. The triangle that surrounds the eye relates to the Holy Trinity, while the rays of light capture the glory of God.

To the Freemasons, the symbol represents guidance from a higher force. It was adopted by the organization in 1797, but adapted slightly, with the removal of the triangle and in some cases the addition of a square and a compass to symbolize the moral virtue of its members.

Universally, the eye is seen as a positive symbol which offers protection, guidance and good fortune to those who work with it.

WORKING WITH EYE OF PROVIDENCE

The third eye is a chakra situated in the middle of the forehead. This energy centre, used in meditation and healing techniques, relates to inner wisdom and intuition. Often linked to the Eye of Providence, the third eye can be opened to help you tap into your intuitive side.

- ❖ *Turn your attention to the area in the centre of your forehead. If it helps, you can lightly trace an eye shape with your finger in this spot, or just picture an eyelid and see it gradually opening.*
- ❖ *Visualize the eye fully open and framed in light.*
- ❖ *See the light extending outward into the world and illuminating your path.*
- ❖ *Relax, and let any thoughts or images flow into your head.*
- ❖ *Trust that your intuitive side will guide you in the right direction.*

PHILOSOPHER'S STONE

KNOWLEDGE,
UNDERSTANDING,
INTUITION

The Philosopher's Stone, was one of the key quests of medieval alchemists, who sought to create a magical substance that would turn lead into gold, and also give the keeper of the stone eternal life. Alchemy was popular in medieval Europe, and a precursor to the more modern practices of chemistry and physics. A science which combines philosophy with the magical arts, it originated in ancient Egypt, Greece and Rome, but had eventually spread throughout Europe by the 12th century.

Alchemists used a range of symbols to represent different scientific elements. These symbols were made up of shapes that contained some of the element's properties, along with celestial influences. They also used these symbols as a way of keeping their research hidden from probing eyes. It was a secret code that helped them document their findings and communicate with each other. For alchemists, the quest to transmute metal into gold was the ultimate goal and while many genuinely studied this, there were those whose only interest was wealth and fame. They turned to cheap magic tricks in the hope of gaining favour, but this gave alchemy a bad name and eventually the science petered out of fashion. Despite this, the symbols remained and became a mainstay in society.

The symbol for the Philosopher's stone is one of the most important as it represents the quest for eternal life and knowledge, holding the key to the universe. Today we know it's not possible to perform feats of magic such as turning lead into gold, but we can use the symbol to help us tune into our intuition and gain a deeper understanding of what makes us tick, which in turn is a kind of precious metal!

WORKING WITH PHILOSOPHER'S STONE

Use the shapes within the Philosopher's Stone symbol to help you tap into your intuition.

❖ *The symbol comprises of three shapes – the circle, the triangle, and the square. Take a large white candle and carve each one of these symbols into the wax.*

❖ *Sprinkle a couple of drops of geranium essential oil on to the candle. This lovely uplifting scent balances the emotions.*

❖ *Light the candle and inhale the sweet aroma.*

❖ *Give your mind the chance to wander and let any thoughts or insights come to you.*

❖ *Let the candle burn down and as you do, make a note of any ideas or thoughts that come into your head.*

WICCA
BLESSING

MOTIVATION,
WISDOM,
INSPIRATION

This blessing is a symbol used by those who follow Wicca, a nature-based religion which has its roots in pre-Christian practices. The word Wicca comes from an Anglo Saxon term which refers to sorcerers, but Wicca is very much linked to the worship of nature and working with the seasons and the earth. A fairly modern path was popularized by Gerald Gardner in the 1940s and 50s — and he is often referred to as the father of Wicca.

The Wiccan Blessing is a crescent-moon-shape from which three tears hang. The moon relates to the moon goddess and is thought to represent her blessing, while the three tears symbolize the three aspects of the triple goddess — the maiden, the mother and the crone. The triple goddess exudes feminine power and wisdom as she embodies the three stages of womanhood. Each tear aligns with a stage, and so the blessing comes imbued with the wisdom of all three.

The moon is important to those who follow Wicca, and any kind of nature-based religion. It is a symbol of light, love and illumination. Linked to the imagination, and the element of water, it governs the emotions and can help us look beyond the surface into the subconscious mind. Its power and light can help us understand our deepest desires and motivations.

The combination of the triple goddess and the moon, makes the blessing a particularly auspicious symbol, and one to work with when you need divine inspiration.

WORKING WITH
WICCA BLESSING

Tap into the invigorating power of the Wicca Blessing by connecting with the feminine element of water.

* *Stand in the shower and let the water rain down on you.*

* *Feel it hit the top of your head and shower you in cleansing drops. Imagine that each drop relates to a tear upon the blessing and an aspect of the triple goddess.*

* *Close your eyes and picture the water imbued with the white light of the moon. Feel this light cleansing you from head to toe, washing away any worries or fears.*

* *Relax and enjoy the sensation of the drops against your skin.*

STRENGTH
AND
PROTECTION

ALGIZ

COURAGE,
PROTECTION,
VISION

Algiz is the one of the Elder Futhark runes, and part of the ancient Nordic alphabet. A powerful symbol with many different meanings, the core essence of this rune is protection. Whether this comes from self-preservation and looking after ourselves, or from the universe and those who care for us. The symbol resembles the branches of a tree stretching up and out to embrace the sun and is thought to represent Yggdrasil, the World Tree in Norse mythology. This mighty Ash extends forth in every direction and carries the weight of the universe upon its branches. It connects and sustains the underworld, the land of the giants and the realm of the gods. Some suggest that Algiz is a direct link to the rainbow bridge known as Bifrost, which runs between this world and Asgard, where the gods reside.

The Ancients believed this symbol was the key to communicating with the gods, whether seeking divine intervention, protection or simply a vision of the future, Algiz could help you reach out to the spiritual realm. A rune with dual elements, it has another name Elhaz, which relates to the element of defence. In this guise the symbol is associated with the elk, a creature that was sacred to the Norse people. To see a white elk was a blessing from the gods and a sign that you were under their protection. As Algiz, the rune is associated with the Swan Maiden, a powerful Valkyrie warrior who sought the brave souls of those who had died in battle.

If you're in need of courage, or simply want to protect yourself from negative thoughts and emotions, Algiz is the symbol to work with.

WORKING WITH ALGIZ

Combine the power of nature with the energy of this symbol for protection and strength.

- ❖ *Sit beneath the boughs of a tree and spend a few moments looking up into the branches. Notice how they spread in every direction, and yet the tree remains strong and rooted to the spot.*
- ❖ *Lean your back against the bark and connect with the energy of the tree. Breathe it in deeply.*
- ❖ *Once you have centred yourself, find three twigs and create the Algiz symbol.*
- ❖ *Spend some time sitting with the symbol you have made.*
- ❖ *Imagine you too are rooted to this spot, just like the tree. You are strong, energized and ready for anything.*

PENTACLE

PROTECTION,
UNITY,
POWER

Set in stone and etched upon monuments, the humble Pentacle has existed since the Stone Age. One of its first proper mentions is in the *Key of Solomon*, a 15th-century grimoire which features dozens of sketches of the symbol. It also appears in the *Heptameron*, a French collection of stories first published in 1558. This five-pointed star encased within a circle might appear simple at first glance, but it's captured hearts and minds across the world and has more recently become a popular pagan symbol. Often mistaken for a Pentagram, the difference between the two comes in the way it is formed — the Pentacle is a star shape framed by a circle, while the Pentagram is a simple continuous line-drawn star with no circle surrounding it.

The Pentacle often crops up as a talisman in magical circles and was thought to be associated with the darker side of witchcraft by those who were scared of the mystical arts. In truth, the Pentacle was a powerful charm used to keep evil at bay and that's how it was used for centuries. The five points of the star have a number of interpretations, although the common belief is that they represent the five elements of earth, air, fire, water and spirit. The circle which surrounds them is a way of showing unity between all the elements and represents the universe.

Early Christians believed the five points were the five wounds that Christ suffered during his crucifixion, while Taoists think they are the five elements of the east, which are wood, water, fire, earth and metal. While the star's points are open to interpretation, the general meaning of this symbol is one of power and protection. Wiccans use it as an emblem of their spiritual practice, representing a connection to the elements and the natural world.

WORKING WITH
PENTACLE

Step into your power and boost your confidence using a technique inspired by this symbol.

- *Stand feet hip-width apart, with your shoulders relaxed.*
- *Lengthen your spine and take a deep breath in.*
- *As you breathe out raise, your arms up and out to make a star shape.*
- *Continue to breathe deeply as you hold the position.*
- *Picture a pentacle just above your navel.*
- *See it shining brightly, filling you with positive energy.*
- *Picture this energy seeping from every pore, making you a beacon of dazzling light.*
- *Draw your arms in a circle down to your sides, then say 'I embrace my personal power'.*

EVIL EYE

TRUTH,
PURITY,
PROTECTION

The Evil Eye has its roots in Mesopotamia, almost 5,000 years ago. It is an ancient symbol, and primarily a curse, which appears in most civilizations and traditions. Eyes, being the windows to the soul, have always been considered highly spiritual and hold a special power that can be used for good and evil. When someone gazes into your eyes, you connect on a deeper level, so it's easy to see how the idea of the Evil-Eye stare found its way into popular culture.

According to folklore, when someone receives the Evil Eye, they will suffer misfortune in some way, from bad luck and illness to the more drastic loss of life. The Evil Eye can be given intentionally, when someone is jealous, or wishes harm to a person, or unintentionally, and there are many folk tales where unsuspecting souls have cut their eyes out to avoid passing the stare on to someone they love.

In some African traditions it's thought that the Evil Eye steals the soul, and so to avoid this some tribes will eat their meals in solitude, as an open mouth makes it easy for the soul to escape. That said, there is a way to banish the curse, and that is with the Evil Eye symbol, which can be worn, carried or hung over doorways.

Usually blue in colour, the symbol is an eye which reflects the bad vibes back to the person who sends them. The light blue hue at the centre of the eye represents the sky and is associated with truth and purity. The symbol is also synonymous with good fortune, and often given as a gift, or a housewarming present.

Today the eye is a source of inspiration for jewellery design and home decor. It's a symbol that can help you repel negative thoughts and remain strong and centred.

WORKING WITH EVIL EYE

Use the image of the Evil Eye in a visualization to keep negative thoughts in check.

❖ *Picture an eye in the centre of your forehead. This eye acts like an antenna when it is fully open, it picks up signals and thoughts and filters them to your brain.*

❖ *Whenever you are feeling negative, or self-critical, turn your attention to the centre of your forehead. See the eye like a giant mirror, reflecting the negative energy away from you.*

❖ *Then, when you're ready, imagine it closing completely and acting as a barrier to harmful thoughts and words.*

TREE OF LIFE

STRENGTH,
CONNECTION,
ROOTED

The tree of life is at the root of many cultures and religions, making it hard to pinpoint its exact origins. An ancient symbol which appears in the bible, in the Book of Genesis, as the tree which grows in the Garden of Eden and sustains all life. It also appears in ancient Egypt, Iran, Mesopotamia and in Celtic mythology. In a way the tree is a universal symbol and something we can all relate to regardless of our culture or belief system.

It is synonymous with growth, strength and peace, but also has a much deeper meaning. The tree has roots and branches which spread outward, and like any tree, it is connected to the rest of the forest, suggesting that we too are connected to each other and that everything that happens is a result of our actions and reactions.

Trees were revered by the Celts, who believed that each one had a spirit and a distinct energy. They were considered sacred and used in rites and rituals. In particular when they cleared the land, they would always leave one tree standing as a symbol to represent that first tree of life, and it was here that they would perform their most powerful rituals.

The tree of life represents our link to nature, how we are born and rooted to the earth, then as we grow, we are nourished by the air and the warming energy of the sun. It is also symbolic of our heritage and signifies the family tree as it branches out in different directions. The links we have to our ancestors, are represented by the network of roots which spread beneath the earth. It's a symbol that reminds us of our roots, and where our true strength lies.

WORKING WITH
TREE OF LIFE

Harness the strength of the Tree of Life
when you need to feel grounded.

---

* *Stand feet hip-width apart. Extend your tailbone and lengthen your spine.*

* *Imagine you are leaning against the trunk of a tree. You feel supported and strong. You look up into the canopy of branches and it reminds you of your connection with nature.*

* *Draw a long deep breath in, and picture roots bursting from the sole of each foot spreading into the earth. Feel these roots curling around the base of the tree and anchoring you in place.*

* *Imagine threads of light extending from the top of your head in every direction, like sprawling branches. They reach out and connect you with friends, family and all the of the people you have yet to meet.*

* *Say 'I am rooted to the earth'.*

TRIQUETRA

STRENGTH,
PROTECTION,
ETERNAL LIFE

The name Triquetra comes from the Latin meaning 'three cornered' and that's the basis of this simple, yet timeless design. It features in Celtic knotwork, upon fabrics and jewellery and is a popular tattoo choice. Although most people assume the Triquetra is of Celtic origin, its roots stem back much further, with appearances in the 4th century BC, where it was found on ceramics in Anatolia and Persia. In Northern Europe it crops up on runestones and early Germanic coins, and it's also been discovered at Indian Heritage sites that are over 5,000 years old.

Its versatility as a symbol, goes some way to explain its popularity with different countries and cultures. While the design is based on three interlacing arcs, the linework is fluid and unbroken which creates a never-ending pattern, this explains the Triquetra's link to eternal life. Although purely decorative, most knots have a purpose, they are used to bind things together and secure them in place so it's understandable the Celts felt it was a symbol of strength and protection. To early Christians the three interconnected arcs represent the Holy Trinity, of the Father, the Son and the Holy Spirit, because of this the

Triquetra is sometimes called the 'Trinity Knot'.

A symbol synonymous with the power of three, it is often linked to the triple goddess, and other aspects of three, like past, present and future, or body, mind and soul. The Celtic concept of land, sea and sky, is also associated with this design, giving rise to the theory that the Triquetra signifies our link with the natural world, which is timeless and eternal.

WORKING WITH TRIQUETRA

Use the Triquetra as your focus with this simple breathing technique to promote strength.

* *Stand or sit in a comfortable position. Place both hands beneath your belly and draw in a deep breath.*

* *Feel your diaphragm rise as you inhale, and then slowly release your outward breath and feel it drop as your chest expands.*

* *Continue to breathe in this way for a couple of minutes, taking note of how your body moves.*

* *Gently interlace your fingers beneath your tummy, to represent the Trinity Knot. This is the seat of your power and strength, where you draw breath into your body.*

* *Sit for a few minutes in this position and continue to focus on your breathing.*

* *As you breath, repeat the affirmation, 'I am strong and energized with every breath.'*

EYE OF HORUS

REJUVENATION,
PROTECTION,
RESILIENCE

A symbol associated with the Egyptian god of the sky Horus; the Eye is thought to hold the power of rejuvenation, it's also synonymous with protection. According to legend, Horus sought revenge for his father's death at the hands of Seth, the god of chaos and storms. The two deities went head to head and a furious battle ensued. During the fight Seth ripped the eye of Horus from his head. Some myths say he tore it into six pieces which he scattered like rubbish, while others suggest it was Horus who gauged his own eye out, as a sacrifice to bring his father back from the dead. Luckily, Hathor, the goddess of magic, was able to restore the eye, transforming it into a symbol of great importance in Egyptian mythology.

Often fashioned into an amulet using precious stones like carnelian and lapis lazuli, each part of the eye is sacred and relates to a different sense. The right side is associated with the sense of smell as it's closest to the nose, the pupil is linked to sight and the eyebrow represents the power of thought. The left side points toward the ear and relates to the sense of hearing, while the curved end, which looks like a stalk of wheat, is linked to taste. Finally, the teardrop symbolizes touch and feeling. Together the parts form the lost eye of Horus and illustrate that whatever happens in life we can overcome, regroup and emerge even stronger. A potent symbol of protection, the Eye of Horus is often painted by fishermen onto boats, as a way to keep them safe during their work. It's a popular talisman and jewellery design, and used as an emblem of strength and resilience.

WORKING WITH
EYE OF HORUS

Recharge your batteries by tapping into the rejuvenating energy of the Eye of Horus.

* *Start by thinking about what you can see right now. It doesn't matter where you are, simply take a moment to enjoy the view and see things as if you're looking at them for the first time.*

* *Next, still your mind and think about what you can hear, from the noises that surround you, to the rhythm of your breathing.*

* *What can you smell? Breathe deeply and inhale the aroma.*

* *Think about what you can taste as you breathe.*

* *Finally, focus on what you can feel, from the clothes you are wearing to how you feel inside.*

* *Your senses should feel enlivened as you engage with the present moment.*

POSITIVE ENERGY

HAMSA

PROTECTION,
STRENGTH,
STABILITY

Also known as the Hand of Fatima, the Hand of Miriam and the Hand of the Goddess, the Hamsa is a hand-shaped symbol with an eye at the centre of the open palm. Often daubed on doors, or hanging above doorways, it's also a popular talisman worn for protection, and thought to repel the Evil Eye. Many cultures have taken the Hamsa to heart, but its origins can be found in ancient Mesopotamia, now Iraq, and Carthage, which is modern Tunisia.

The Arabic word for Hamsa is 'Khamsah' meaning 'five', and this number is highly symbolic in the Muslim faith. There are five pillars of Islam and Thursday is known as the fifth day — the best time to perform rites and rituals for protection. The 'five' also refers to the five fingers of the right hand which form the Hamsa. Depending on how the fingers are displayed, the symbol has slightly different connotations. Widely spread digits are thought to attract good luck, while fingers that are closer together dispel negativity.

Hugely popular in Arabic and Berber culture, the Hamsa, along with the number 'five' is used to keep harmful energy at bay, and the symbol itself appears in the national emblem for Algeria.

The Hamsa inspires many interior designers and is used in home furnishings and decor, as well as ornate jewellery. While the symbol can be any colour, hues of vibrant blue and green tend to be favoured as this is thought to represent the eyes of God and exude heavenly power. A symbol that provides strength, protection and a shield from negative energy, it can also fortify your inner core and help you find stability amid chaos.

WORKING WITH
HAMSA

Use the protective energy of the Hamsa to restore balance and boost your self-esteem.

❖ *On a piece of paper, trace around your hand, then draw a circle in the centre of the palm. This area represents who you are and how you would like to feel.*

❖ *In the circle, write down a word to represent this, for example, if you want to feel happy, you could write 'joyful'.*

❖ *Along each finger write one thing you can do to help you feel that way. This could be a simple change in attitude, like thinking positively, or something more practical like taking up a new form of exercise.*

❖ *Position your Hamsa-inspired drawing somewhere that you will see it every day, like on a noticeboard, or near your workspace to remind you that you have the power to change your life.*

TIBETAN KNOT

HARMONY,
UNITY,
CONNECTION

Also known as the 'endless' or 'glorious' knot, this interwoven design has no beginning or end, giving it a timeless and powerful energy. Thought to date back to 2500 BC when it first appeared on clay tablets in the Indus Valley. One of eight auspicious symbols relayed to Buddha after he attained enlightenment, the interconnecting loops represent endless wisdom and compassion. The way the shapes weave into each other suggests that everything in the universe is connected, there is no separation, we are interdependent, and exist as one.

A popular symbol in Tibet, it is also associated with good fortune and often woven into mats, carpets and prayer flags. Ceremonial scarves known as Khatas use the pattern of this knot in their colourful designs, as do decorative door hangings. The key theme of this symbol is universal harmony, and this is illustrated by the fact that there are no gaps between the patterns. The closeness of the lines and the way they flow, signify the binding of karmic destinies and the underlying reality of existence, so this symbol often appears on gift cards, as a way of bringing the giver and the receiver together.

A symbol of unity and love, it can be used to promote harmony within the home, at work and in the wider community. It can also help you deepen the connection you have with others.

WORKING WITH
TIBETAN KNOT

Use the fortuitous energy of this symbol to spread loving energy within your environment.

- ❖ *Take the Tibetan knot and reproduce it on a large piece of paper.*
- ❖ *Spend some time sitting with the image and thinking about all that it represents.*
- ❖ *Place your hands on the paper and imagine you are breathing in light and love. As you breathe out, imagine that you're pouring all of that positive energy into the symbol through your hands.*
- ❖ *Give yourself a few moments to feel relaxed and recharged, then take the paper and fold it up.*
- ❖ *Place it somewhere near your front door to attract positive energy into your home. You can also position the image in your office, at work, or anywhere else that you spend a lot of time.*

ITALIAN HORN

FERTILITY, GOOD FORTUNE, PROTECTION

The Italian horn, otherwise known as the Cornicello, is an ancient symbol thought to offer protection against the Evil Eye. It originates from the Neolithic period, when the people of the Mediterranean used it as a symbol of fertility and good fortune. At the time horns, particularly those of the bull, were thought to be imbued with virility so anything horn-shaped was associated with strength and fertility. The Ancients adopted the Cornicello and used it in votives and offerings to the Roman goddess of love Venus, and also to Luna, the goddess of the moon.

Over time, the symbol evolved and was thought to repel evil and attract good fortune. Fashioned into charms and amulets using red coral, silver and bone, it's a common sight in the city of Naples. Red horns have extra magical power, as red is the colour of victory and love. The shape and bright hue resemble the chilli pepper — a common symbol of good luck in Naples — while silver horns are imbued with the power of the goddess Luna. The curved silhouette also adds to the meaning and is described in Italian as 'tuosto, stuorto e cu a' punta' which translates as 'tough and twisted at the tip'.

Today you'll find horns strewn from gateposts and hung in doorways to protect those who live there. Shops often have them hanging near the entrance to attract more custom and they're also tied to rear-view mirrors in cars to keep the passengers safe.

WORKING WITH
ITALIAN HORN

Make the Italian horn your good-luck charm, and a tool to help you move toward your goals.

- *The twisty outline of the horn reflects your journey to success. It isn't always a straight path, but if you want to achieve your dreams, you have to learn to go with the flow.*

- *Spend some time thinking about a recent achievement and consider how you reached that point. Did you have to adapt your thinking? Were you flexible in the choices you made?*

- *Now think about your next goal, and rather than planning every step, see yourself achieving this dream. Imagine how you'll feel when you get there and conjure those happy emotions.*

- *By focusing on a positive outcome, you create a positive outlook which will help you move forward. Whenever you need to switch up your thinking, bring the Italian horn to mind and it will remind you of the fluid path to success.*

HORSESHOE

L U C K ,
P R O T E C T I O N ,
B L E S S I N G

The horseshoe has long been a symbol of good luck and protection. During the Middle Ages it was common practice to come across discarded horseshoes, as almost every village had a blacksmith. The lucky finder of a shoe would hang it above the door to keep evil at bay, and attract good fortune. It was a popular belief that iron held magical properties and could repel witches and fairies, but the original reason for the shoe's power dates back to 959 AD and the tale of St Dunstan and the Devil.

While there are many variations of the narrative, the basic tale tells of Dunstan's meeting with the Devil, and how during their final encounter, Dunstan nailed a horseshoe to his cloven hoof. Howling in pain the Devil cried for help, but Dunstan only agreed to remove the shoe if the Devil promised not to darken his door, or any door with a horseshoe nailed above it. From this point onward the horseshoe was considered a lucky charm, and an effective way to keep harmful spirits at bay.

How you hang the horseshoe impacts its meaning. An upward-turned shoe in the shape of a U acts like a lucky bowl, catching good fortune, while a downward-turned horseshoe showers those who pass beneath it with luck. The curved profile also has some bearing on its meaning. In ancient Europe it was associated with the crescent moon, which meant it was blessed with lunar power.

WORKING WITH
HORSESHOE

According to folklore, it's best to stumble upon a horseshoe, or be given one as a gift, but visualizing one can also help you switch your attitude to one of gratitude.

❖ *Picture an upturned horseshoe above your head, and just like the ancients, imagine it's filled with wonderful blessings.*

❖ *Go through each one in your mind, making a list of all the things that you are thankful for. Anything from your close relationships and friendships to the air you breathe and the earth you walk upon.*

❖ *Try and think of at least ten things to sit in your horseshoe and carry with you. Whenever you feel negative thoughts surfacing, remind yourself of the horseshoe of blessings above your head.*

❖ *Perform this mini visualization at the beginning of every day to put you in a positive mindset and remember to add new things to your horseshoe of blessings.*

FLOWER OF LIFE

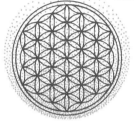

CREATION,
LIFE,
PROPORTION

The Flower of Life is an ancient symbol which features in cultures around the world. The earliest known depictions were discovered in the Temple of Osiris in Egypt and are thought to be 6,000 years old. Made from red ochre burnt onto granite, it's believed they were crafted as a representation of the Eye of Horus (page 96–97).

The flower appears in ancient texts, museums and also architecture, but it wouldn't be given its official moniker as the Flower of Life, until the 1990s. Even so, it caused a wave of fascination which lasted thousands of years. Leonardo da Vinci was captivated by the form and studied it in great detail. From this he derived the Golden Ratio of Phi and the five platonic solids. Others have linked the geometric symbol to the Kabbalah, a form of esoteric Judaism, and believe that the Tree of Life stems from the original flower.

Nineteen overlapping circles create the base for the symmetrical blooms, which are evenly spaced and in perfect proportion, although there are variations with as little as seven circles. The flower in the centre is thought to represent the source of life, while the symbol as a whole depicts the cycle of creation. The sacred pattern of the universe is thought to lie at the heart of the symbol, giving those who can read and understand it the divine knowledge of all creation.

Today the flower appears in designs for tattoos, and in decor and jewellery, but there are still those who study its many facets in the hope of discovering the key to the universe.

WORKING WITH
FLOWER
OF LIFE

Take inspiration from the Flower of Life and use it as the basis for an exercise in finding joy.

❖ *On a sheet of paper, draw a circle to represent the centre of the flower. This also represents you and what's most important in your life right now. When you've completed the circle, colour it in, in a shade that matches how you feel about things at the present moment.*

❖ *Next, create the petals by drawing loops around the outside. Within each petal write a few words to describe something that brings you joy every day, like your morning coffee, or listening to your favourite song.*

❖ *Each day make a point of doing at least one of the things you've written in the petals.*

METATRON'S CUBE

CREATIVITY,
BALANCE,
DIVINE

According to myth, this complex two-dimensional shape was born from the soul of the Archangel Metatron. Belonging to one of the highest ranks of angels associated with God, Metatron is thought to be the angel of life and a sacred scribe. He governs the flow of energy to all things and helps bridge the connection to the Divine. The cube is thought to contain every shape which exists in the universe. It is a blueprint for life on earth and as such holds the building blocks from which God created the world and everything in it. It is Metatron's responsibility to ensure there's a constant flow of energy to all parts of the cube. In doing so he keeps the natural world in order and everything in balance.

The geometric shapes within the cube are known as the Platonic Solids, thanks to Plato who linked them to the spiritual world. They are thought to represent every earthly form from snowflakes and crystals to our DNA.

The cube holds the secret to life, and how we were made, making it a symbol synonymous with creative energy. It's thought that studying the intricate patterns can bring a deeper understanding of how we work, from the way the body and soul fits together to our place in the world. It's also believed that the cube can help banish negative thoughts and restore positive energy. It spins in a clockwise direction and pushes away negativity, while helping to heal and balance our energy centres.

WORKING WITH
METATRON'S CUBE

Use the power of Metatron's Cube to switch up your thoughts and focus on the positive aspects in your life.

❖ *Look at an image of Metatron's Cube. Lose yourself in the patterns and let them take you on a journey.*

❖ *What do they remind you of in the real world? Perhaps you can see flowers within the symbol, or maybe it reminds you of a gathering of stars, or a cluster of snowflakes. Let your imagination wander and enjoy picturing these wonders of nature.*

❖ *Now think about the beauty in your own world and consider the everyday things that make you smile. What makes you feel good inside?*

❖ *Repeat this exercise several times over a few weeks.*

❖ *Eventually just looking at the symbol will help you feel more positive.*

HEALING

TWO GOLDEN FISH

ENLIGHTENMENT,
BALANCE,
LOYALTY

Vibrant and perfectly matched, these two golden fish bring prosperity and healing when they swim into your life. Originally linked to the two main rivers of India, the Ganges and Yamuna, these channels of water were sacred to the people who lived on the banks, helping to sustain and nourish them. In addition they were thought to represent the lunar and solar channels of the nostrils, which determine the rhythm of each life-giving breath.

In Buddhism they are one of eight auspicious symbols which represent the enlightened mind. Their symmetry is a reflection of the dance between intellect and emotion, and how finding the balance between the two can bring true happiness, while the freedom of swimming in the ocean brings even deeper joy. In Hinduism the god Vishnu transformed into a fish and saved humanity from a flood, so the fish is seen as a sacred and gracious creature.

Being a pair, the fish are thought to symbolize loyalty and harmony within couples. Fertility is highlighted too as fish multiply quickly. This coupled with the idea that they are together forever makes them a fortuitous omen for newlyweds and those wishing to have children.

With these many positive connotations, it's easy to see why the symbol of two golden fish has inspired jewellery design and decor. Working with this symbol can help you recharge your batteries, boost positive energy and heal body and mind.

WORKING WITH
TWO GOLDEN FISH

Tap into the healing energy of the golden fish with an easy visualization.

- ❖ *Visualize yourself floating in a golden pool shaped like the symbol.*
- ❖ *Close your eyes and breathe deeply. Relax your shoulders and feel the weightlessness of your body.*
- ❖ *Imagine ripples of golden light emanating from the water and bathing you in vibrant energy.*
- ❖ *As you inhale, the light seeps beneath your skin and fills you up with warmth and vitality.*
- ❖ *Say 'With every breath, I am healed'.*

HARTH

L O V E ,
N U R T U R I N G ,
B A L A N C E

The Harth symbol has its roots in Karuna Reiki, a form of healing which taps into universal energy and works with the chakras, the energy centres in the body. Karuna Reiki differs from standard Reiki, as it works at a higher vibrational level and focuses on the loving energy of the heart. Reiki first came into being in mid-19th century Japan as a type of hands-on energy healing, but Karuna Reiki was developed in 1995 by Master William Lee Rand and some of his students. This type of Reiki has forgiveness and compassion at its core.

The Harth symbol represents the path to unconditional love and can be used to heal all types of relationship, including the one we have with ourselves. It represents love in its purest form, and helps us connect with others and the Divine from the heart. Thought to embody the nurturing energy of the Mother Goddess, Harth is also associated with Guan Yin, the Buddhist deity who is known for her compassionate spirit.

To activate the power of Harth, a practitioner will either visualize the symbol, draw or trace it over the body, or speak its name. In doing this, they harness the specific energy of the symbol and direct the healing to the area it's needed.

Harth is the perfect symbol to restore body and mind. It can help balance the emotions, soothe turmoil and heartbreak, and also open the heart so that love can flow freely.

WORKING WITH HARTH

Combine the power of Harth with aromatherapy for a self-healing practice that will soothe your soul.

- ❖ *Sit quietly and spend a few minutes breathing deeply to clear your mind.*

- ❖ *When you're ready, dab a couple of drops of lavender essential oil onto your fingers and begin marking out the Harth symbol on your chest. Don't worry if the symbol is not an exact match, just focus on the meaning of the symbol and your own intention to heal yourself.*

- ❖ *Breathe deeply and take in the soothing aroma of the lavender oil as you do this.*

- ❖ *When you've finished creating the symbol, relax and imagine that with every breath in, you are sending healing energy to your heart.*

INFINITY

UNITY,
LOVE,
HARMONY

The infinity symbol, also called the Forever symbol, has its roots in mathematics, which is no surprise when you consider it looks like the number 8 on its side. It first appeared in 1655, when the mathematician John Wallis decided to use it to represent infinity. It's thought that he was inspired by the Roman numeral for 'many' which looks similar. He's not the only mathematician to have dabbled with this symbol. It also crops up in the works of Leonhard Euler, who used it to mark 'absolute infinity'.

Although it was brought to the attention of the masses through maths, its origins go back much further to the Ouroboros, a symbol which appears in Egyptian and Greek mythology. The Ouroboros (pages 20–21) is a snake that devours its own tail, creating a never-ending loop which represents eternity and the cycle of life and death. This fits with the infinity symbol, which also represents a never-ending cycle, the lines being forever entwined. The two loops of the sideways figure of eight suggest there is unity with this symbol. It's about two elements coming together to form one, and as such it's a popular emblem for love. Even without the romantic influence, it's a symbol of harmony and balance.

In Hinduism the infinity symbol stands for Kundalini energy, which is represented as a coiled serpent at the base of the spine. In Christianity it relates to God, and his everlasting presence, while some believe it sums up the nature of universe which is in continual motion.

WORKING WITH INFINITY

Use the power of the infinity symbol to help you release something, like a bad habit, a memory or a person that is no longer good for you.

- ❖ *Close your eyes and picture the infinity symbol outlined in bright light on the floor.*

- ❖ *See yourself standing in one loop of the symbol. In the other loop is an image which sums up the thing or person that you wish to let go of.*

- ❖ *Breathe deeply and picture the symbol slowly fading. It gets lighter and lighter until it completely disappears from sight.*

- ❖ *Acknowledge that you are no longer locked in an eternal loop and can release what you don't need by saying a few words such as 'I release you, I am free to move forward'.*

BRIGID'S CROSS

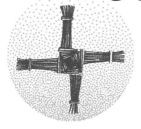

FERTILITY,
HEALING,
GROWTH

Traditionally made in Ireland to mark St Brigid's day, which falls on the 1st February, the cross appears to be a Christian Symbol, but its roots go back to Pagan times, and the goddess Brigid.

Saint Brigid was the founder of the first monastery in Kildare, and the first female patron saint of Ireland, while in her earlier guise as a Gaelic goddess, she governs poets, artists and healers, and is often associated with childbirth and inspiration. Also known as

the goddess of fire, she's linked to the hearth. Her cross, which is usually fashioned from rushes with a square of material at the centre and four radials, was hung on the kitchen wall to protect the house from fire and evil spirits — a practice which is still popular today in rural Ireland.

While the 1st marks Saint Brigid's feast day, it is also the start of Imbolc, the pagan festival which celebrates the coming of spring. The name Imbolc comes from the Irish word meaning 'in the belly', a nod to the theme of fertility, and the womb of the earth slowly coming to life.

As a symbol of Imbolc, the cross signifies the first glimpse of spring, when young shoots burst forth in search of the warmth and light of the sun. A cornerstone of the Celtic year, Imbolc meant the earth was ripening, nature was starting to wake up and new growth was afoot. It was a time to give thanks for the return of longer, lighter days and to make plans for future harvests.

Brigid's Cross can help the light return to your world, from renewed hope to inspiration and fertility, it is a symbol synonymous with healing.

WORKING WITH BRIGID'S CROSS

Use the healing energy of Brigid's Cross to attract positivity into your home. This exercise is particularly effective when carried out on or near the 1st February.

* *Take an image of the cross, or recreate it yourself, by tracing it onto some paper.*

* *Next, find a pretty vase and fill it with spring blooms like bluebells, tulips and crocuses.*

* *Place the vase on the top of the symbol and put it somewhere near the entrance to your home.*

* *Make sure that there are no obstructions near the entrance and that it is clean and free from clutter, which can obstruct the flow of positive energy into your home.*

* *Open the windows and welcome in nature's healing energy.*

* *Refresh the flowers with clean water every day and give thanks for the rejuvenating energy of spring.*

INGUZ

RENEWED HOPE,
REBIRTH,
GROWTH

Known as the 'Divine Seed' or the Norse god Ing, this rune is the starting point of all things. It is the seedling from which great ideas grow. Part of the Runic alphabet, popular with Germanic tribes of Northern Europe and Scandinavia, Inguz is known as the seed rune, and as such represents new beginnings. It's a symbol of masculine energy and life-force, the seed that is nurtured and becomes the sapling, the shoot and finally the seasoned tree.

Associated with the god Ing, also known as Freyr or Frey in Norse mythology. He is the god of peace and fertility and also linked to sunshine and rain, making him a key part of the harvesting process.

When this rune shows up in a reading it relates to a new phase of life, or a beginning of sorts. It's the idea that comes from out of nowhere and leads to great things, the creative energy that drives us forward. It's also associated with peace and harmony. There's a link to family with this rune too, as the name Ing derives from the Proto-Germanic word for 'ancestor', so the symbol is synonymous with inherited gifts, and the knowledge passed on from those who have gone before us.

Symmetrical in style and shape, Inguz is often depicted with just the central diamond shape on show. It can be used as a blessing, and to infuse other objects with healing power.

WORKING WITH
INGUZ

Use the basic shape of Inguz to sow seeds for health and vitality with a simple gardening ritual.

❖ *Choose the type of seeds you'd like to grow. Go for something edible like vegetables or herbs.*

❖ *Pick your pot and fill it with enough soil for the seeds.*

❖ *Place the seeds in a dish in front of you. Spend a few minutes breathing deeply to calm and focus the mind, then place your hands together, fingers and thumbs touching to create the central diamond shape of the Inguz symbol.*

❖ *Let this hover over the dish of seeds. Breathe in and as you exhale, imagine light and energy infusing the seeds with the power of Inguz. When you are ready, place the seeds in the soil, cover, then water.*

❖ *Repeat this exercise each time you tend to the seeds.*

HALU

EMPATHY,
CONNECTION,
STRENGTH

A symbol used by Karuna Reiki practitioners, Halu has the ability to enhance the healing process, and prevent negative thought patterns from developing. Karuna Reiki has compassion at its heart and uses the power of love and forgiveness to accelerate healing. While it is hands on, it also involves verbal chanting and visualizing a range of symbols which direct the healing energy. The word 'Karuna' comes from a Sanskrit word, which embodies empathic action toward another, and this sums up the practice perfectly. Those who engage in this type of Reiki connect with the pain of the person they are working with in order to help them.

Halu, which has a pyramid-type structure, is used as a shield to protect against harmful energy entering the body and mind. It encases the receiver in light and prevents emotional and psychic attack. Particularly useful in situations where a person is feeling vulnerable and manipulated, Halu can provide a safe place from which they can heal and find the strength to move forward. Often used in conjunction with Zonar, the first symbol of Karuna Reiki, which focuses on healing trauma and painful memories.

Halu is also thought to repel the Evil Eye and any form of negative energy sent in your direction. The top of the symbol that forms a pyramid is like a protective cap which keeps the mind safe from self-criticism and the critical thoughts of others.

WORKING WITH
HALU

Use Halu as a shield to keep negative thoughts at bay.

- ❖ *Position the symbol at eye level and spend some time gazing at it. Don't rush the process, simply enjoy being in the presence of the symbol. Skim over the shape with your eyes until you feel you know every part of it.*

- ❖ *When you're ready, close your eyes and imagine the Halu above your head.*

- ❖ *The symbol exudes a pyramid of protective light, which covers you from head to toe.*

- ❖ *When you breathe in, you breathe in this vibrant light, when you breathe out you release any negative thoughts and emotions.*

- ❖ *Wherever you go, and whatever you're doing, the symbol remains a comforting presence that you can call on. All you have to do is visualize the pyramid of light showering you with healing energy.*

ANKH

LOVE,
LIFE,
REJUVENATION

The Ankh is a cross with a loop at the top which was often embellished with other decorations. Simplistic in its original form and shape, it is one of the most popular and powerful symbols associated with ancient Egypt. Dating from the Early Dynastic Period (c. 3150−2613 BCE) it was engraved in tombs or worn as an amulet. Synonymous with eternal life, it represents the soul's journey upon the earth and then on to the afterlife.

The hieroglyph means 'the breath of life' and is yet another nod to the cycles of birth, life, death and beyond.

The origins of this symbol are sketchy, but some believe that the idea of the Ankh evolved from the sandal, the looped top being the strap which wraps around the ankle, while the straight line is the sole keeping the wearer secure. This modest footwear was essential to the ancient Egyptians, helping them navigate a path through life, just as the ankh could assist and protect those who bore it. Other scholars believe that the Ankh formed a part of the belt belonging to the goddess of magic, Isis. In this respect, it was often thought of as a fertility symbol. Either way, the Ankh was revered and associated with vitality, strength and the promise of new life.

A favourite of the god of the afterlife, Anubis, who was often pictured placing it to the lips of departed souls to bring them back from the dead, the ankh carries potent energy that can be used to revitalize and rejuvenate body and mind. It promotes strength and the capacity for renewal.

WORKING WITH ANKH

Use the shape of the Ankh as a meditation tool to focus your mind and draw life-giving energy with each breath.

- ❖ *Stand with your shoulders back, feet hip-width apart and your chin tilted up.*
- ❖ *Tuck your tailbone in and extend your spine.*
- ❖ *Take a deep breath in and imagine you are drawing it up through your feet, along your legs and spine and then over the top of your head, in a loop.*
- ❖ *As you exhale, carry the breath down over the front of your body and back through your feet into the earth.*
- ❖ *See yourself as a physical representation of the Ankh and carry on with this breathing cycle for a few minutes.*
- ❖ *Every time you inhale, you draw energy from the earth. Every time you exhale, you return it to the ground.*